BECAUSE THE OTHER KID GOT HIT BY A BUS

!!

BECAUSE THE OTHER KID GOT HIT BY A BUS

Turn challenges into opportunities and become the person you were meant to be.

Angie Gleine

Library of Congress Cataloging-in-Publication Data is available.

ISBN-13: 9781098575595

Dedication

To my family and friends who have lit the fire, pushed me out of my comfort zone and supported my every breath. Each word I write comes from my happily beating heart and every beat is because of you.

For those of us who are just starting to become the person we are meant to be. Those passionate souls that feel in their bones they are meant for more. If you're thinking, I'm not special enough, I'm not brave enough or who am I to do something great? I'm telling you that you are enough, and this is proof. This book is for you.

Table of Contents

Just a Spec

I am no doctor, not even close. However, I am a lot of things. I am a daughter, sister, mom, wife, and friend, who is overly sensitive, feisty, and imperfect: I am YOU. At least a little bit.

I also live with chronic pain, every freaking day. The type of pain that leaves you unable to squeeze the damn toothpaste or tie your shoes. The type of pain that leaves you dependent on heavy medications that you know are rotting your insides. But this pain often feels like you are stripped of the gift of CHOICE. And while you are swallowing the pills, or having them injected, you are thinking – ok, so the pain is manageable, but for how long? What about the long-term quality of my life? Am I going to get stronger symptoms down the road? Will it lead to other autoimmune diseases? Or, even worse, will it cause a terminal disease? And THAT makes me angry. I am choosing to turn my anger into opportunity.

ENOUGH!

"Actually, I just woke up one day and decided I didn't want to feel like that anymore, or ever again. So, I changed. Just. Like. That." ~ Unknown.

I realize that I cannot change my DNA. I cannot change that fact that I am living a life with Rheumatoid Arthritis, Colitis, Alopecia Areata and imperfect children with an imperfect marriage. But I have a CHOICE on how I live my life.

I CHOOSE HAPPY.

Every day. Every night. With every breath. Why? Because I can. There are people who cannot fight their diseases, or their children's' diseases. How lucky am I to have to ability to CHOOSE how I handle my imperfections? I shifted my brain and thought, "Ok, well this sucks. Kind of a shitty DNA deal here. But – I am living with chronic pain, not dying with it."

So, let's do something about it. No pouting. No "poor me."

Live with the pain – because what is the other option? Not one I am willing to choose.

Chronic pain is a lot like erosion. It's real and it is happening. You have beautiful surroundings, but due to elements out of your control, the structure changes. It withers away as if it is destroying itself. There are measures you can take to prevent or slow down the progression of the erosion. You can meet with all the fancy specialists, experiment with all the bizarre diet trends and do all the research.

However, erosion cannot be stopped. But if you look closely, sometimes treasures can be discovered. New beginnings and new learning opportunities are unearthed if you are open to seeing it. The soil or roots may give way and look altered. You will stumble and slip. So, look for the shiny stone, the rare fossils or artifacts that now become part of who you are because I promise you, they are in there. But you have to dig. You have to put in the work. And only you can make the choice.

Choose to look past the bullshit of erosion. Choose to see the treasure in there. It's happening every day, like it or not. Accept it as part of your nature and turn this new treasure into an opportunity to grow stronger, love deeper and be even more grateful.

This is my story. A story of the power of perspective, turning challenges into opportunities and playing the hell out of the cards you've been dealt. But mostly, it's a story of choosing happiness and ultimately having the courage to become who you were meant to be.

The Story of the Bus

So, um, that's an aggressive title.

I feel like I owe you lovely readers an explanation for choosing such a shocking title. I think you'll find it to be a heartbreakingly beautiful story on the power of perspective.

Is there anything more difficult than watching your child suffer in pain? When my daughter was three, there were a few weeks when she was complaining about her knee hurting. After picking her up from preschool, one morning, she reminded me about the pain. Most parents would associate it with growing pains and be able to shrug it off. However, since I worry more than I need to about most things, I diagnosed Lucy with juvenile rheumatoid arthritis and started researching her medications before even consulting her doctor. I was diagnosed with juvenile rheumatoid arthritis at three years old, so it's very practical of me to diagnose her as well. This is what most people call "overthinking the situation." I realize this is not rational behavior, however, this is the way my brain works. I am what I am. Mama knows best, right?

In my mind, I was stressing over the long-term effects of all her medications and how they would affect her life. OMG! What if she is on hundreds of meds before she turns ten? What if they stunt her growth or mental development? We need a team of specialists S.T.A.T. I had called both of my parents before we even drove home from preschool to get their opinion on raising a child with arthritis. Mind you, the drive from her preschool to our house is approximately 3.2 miles. It does not take a physiologist to realize that I was totally assuming that my daughter would inherit my DNA and be diagnosed at three, simply because I was. In reality, she had no pain the next day and has not complained about it since. She probably bumped it on a chair or the playground like the brilliant, beautiful, clumsy child she is.

While calling my dad in a panic that morning, I asked him how he handled having a child with chronic pain. So many doctors' appointments, pokes and pricks and WAITING for results. Both my parents, doing divorce and co-parenting at its finest, were hanging in there with me every step of the way. The blood draws were the worst. I mean, the worst. I was anxious, teary, hole in the stomach kind of terrified every single time. I actually still have a hard time with needles, and I've had thousands injected over the years. I remember being bribed with money, Happy Meals and ice cream if I wouldn't cry and could just hold it together. I'm not sure I ever did, but I always got the prize at the end.

My favorite bribe was a bright purple pen my dad had in this shirt pocket. Man, it was the most beautiful purple pen a 3rd grade girl had ever seen. I would have done anything to call it my own. Imagine the notes I could write to my friends and the pictures I could doodle during class! The deal was- no crying, and I get the pen. I was determined not to back down. Fear would NOT win over the power of the purple pen! It would be mine! Well, I still cried, but I gave it my all while the nurses held my arm down and I turned my head. They were tears of bravery and determination, with a side of horror and mild traumatization. Damn needles. In the end, I got the pen, they got their blood. Everybody wins.

It was during this phone call that all the memories of the constant rotating door of hospital visits came flooding back. I did not want to go through this as a parent! It was hard enough as a child. So, my dad, who is a fighter through and through, had some pretty simple advice. "Because some other kid had gotten hit by a bus." Calm demeanor and tone in his voice.

Huh? A bus? A kid got hit by a bus? Did you hear my question, dad?

Now, I should explain that my dad worked at Children's Hospital in Dayton, Ohio where my doctor's appointments were. So, he saw and heard the worst of the worst when it came to children. He went on to tell me that he had just left the ER before heading to one of my appointments. In the ER on that particular day, he had been asked to intubate a young boy. As my dad began the quick procedure, he could see that little boys' chances of survival were very slim. After asking what this poor boy had been through, the medical team reported that he had sadly been hit by a bus. Tragically, as expected his injuries were so severe that he was unable to survive them.

How's that for perspective? Imagine those parents and family members?

So even though my dad had worries, concerns and unanswered questions, I had not been hit by a bus. My little 3-year-old heart was beating, my blood was pumping, and my lungs were breathing. I was alive. Stressful and struggling, yes. But alive. I was raised with that powerful perspective.

From that point on, as a patient and as a mother, I flipped a switch in my thinking. I may be dealing with chronic pain; my daughter may end up dealing with chronic pain. There might be an endless number of doctors, pokes and pricks, and time spent awaiting test results. But the pain is NOT a bus.

It's not an end. It's an eviction from your current health, yet an invitation to fight it with grace. I GET to fight. I have an opportunity.

I do realize that this is a strong message. It is not for the faint of heart. However, the message is full of hope, perseverance and the reality that things aren't as bad as they seem. There is a post-it hanging in my kitchen even today saying, "Because the other kid got hit by a bus". It reminds me that I start the day in pain, overwhelmed, or stressed, but at least I start each day. That's the power of perspective and the story of "The Bus."

Chapter One: You'll Feel Better if You Curl Your Hair and Other Life Lessons

Backing It Up Real Quick

'm mostly a good girl. Not exactly what you would call "precious," which I'll talk more about later, but a good girl. I'm often the lady at Giant Eagle who will take not only my shopping cart, but all the lonely surrounding carts in the parking lot and return them to their rightful home in the cart corral. I have a hard time understanding why you wouldn't return your grocery cart! Yet I'm also the girl who shares snarky, inappropriate comments under her breath. Usually involving swear words. So, see? Nobody is perfect.

However, it's important you know that I'm a rule follower. It probably drove my older brother nuts knowing that he grew up much less concerned about the world's approval. I, on the other hand, needed to know you were proud of me in order to not crumble to keep my head above water. Please, just like me and tell me how great I am, or I might fall apart. Somehow our balanced personalities worked for us. He is my only fully biological sibling allowing us to be partners in crime and have each other's backs. Snow days were spent playing "hot lava," jumping from one piece of furniture to the next. When you have single, working parents you are able to get away with things like this. There was not a whole lot of fighting between us outside of watching "Grease" versus the Bengals or Celtics. And the time he and a buddy left a self-breast exam brochure on my bedroom door. Which you could imagine the humiliation I felt as a 5th grader when your 7th grade brother and friend leave that for you!

When there was a disagreement, I usually got my way because I was the rule follower. I learned early on that following the rules was safe, and usually got you what you wanted. I was not about to rock the boat or make waves. I wanted everyone to be calm and life to be easy breezy. Which is fairly simple when you're 10 growing up in a safe, small suburb in Columbus, Ohio.

I'm not sure why I needed so much reinforcement. I was fortunate to grow up with two loving, yet divorced, parents. As a young child I did not grow up seeing what a traditional marriage looked like and based my model on the Huxtable's from "The Cosby Show", which seemed like a good idea at the time, but know I'm doubting that, too. I had a beautiful childhood with everything I needed, even if my school clothes were on lay-a-way from KMART, I didn't know anything else. I also have the best memories of my Grandmom taking the girl cousins shopping at City Center downtown or Schottenstein's, also known as "Schotty's" to the family. Every year she spent the day making us feel fancy and significant as if showing us what we were worthy of. I knew, even from my earliest days, I had people in my life that would surround me with love, support and laughter. However, I always felt a little different, a little too sensitive, undeserving and scared about the world around me. As if at any moment, everything and everyone I love could be taken from me. Even all these years later, that same feeling that I used to shove down as a little girl tucked under my yellow lacy comforter, can still come creeping in. However, I hold the power over those fears now.

I knew from an early age that my parents had to work really hard as single co-parents. There are many families who make their divorce struggle public, but I have no memories of arguments between my parents. Isn't that crazy? I went back and forth between my various grandparents and cousins touring Ohio in my traveling circus of co-parenting. We had family vacations on the beach, week-long sleepovers with cousins from Cincinnati, Columbus and down to Portsmouth. Swimming, sewing, countless skits and homemade baked goods filled my memory bank. There was love around every corner. It wasn't traditional, but it was mine and it was enough. I realize it sounds like an annoying made for TV movie. You may want to watch out for it on Hallmark or Lifetime next fall. I'm sure they are working on the screenplay as we speak. I knew I was lucky from an early age. My Brady Bunch vibes were spread across the state of Ohio.

At the same time, however, keep in mind that my brother is two years older than me and may remember things a little differently. His memories include a clearer image of the impact divorce has on children. But I was three during this time and grew up with my own version of "normal." Both my parents came to conferences together, parents' nights, plays and negotiated car rides to my dance studio. They made it look mostly seamless. So, I think I learned at an early age not to complain and to make things look easy. My brother, who is one of my favorite people, has the heart of a giant. He grew up willing to push and pull in order to get his way. He is an intense spirit who fights for what he believes. Maybe it's because he has seen more pain than me, or maybe it's just who he was born to be. Either way, I knew that pain and sadness was an overwhelming weight that could take me down. It was too much for me. Remember as a kid, playing that parachute game in gym class? It was the best, right? Everyone was standing in a circle holding the colorful parachute, then you raise your arms in unison so that it balloons up in a bubble. Next, everyone steps inside the inflated dome and quickly sits down on the edges, right? Imagine sitting under there alone as it slowly falls on your head, your arms and your legs as the air gradually slips out. That is the overwhelming suffocation of pain.

Hold up! Wait a minute! I grew up with love and support and all the things children need to feel good about who they are. There's no reason why I shouldn't be confident and strong! It has taken me many years, failures and embarrassing moments to realize that I find comfort in control. It's my comfort zone. My safe place. It's where no one's feathers will be ruffled. No pushing and pulling for me. I was well into my adult, married life when I came to terms with this reality. I remember turning to my husband in the car and saying, "I think I have a hard time when I cannot control things."

You guys, he laughed at me. Not necessarily in a hurtful way. More like I was asking him if he knew about the instability of the Middle East. Apparently, everyone was well informed, and I was the last to know. How did I not know? Why was I the last to the party? Especially when "the party" was my life! It's not as if I was taught or encouraged to be a control freak. My life made it easy to have control. Growing up in a single sibling house, (I was fortunate to gain two half-sisters in my teenage years) with two working parents meant I had to do a lot for myself and I mean that in the best way. It was up to me to make sure my homework was done, my lunch was packed and that I was not a burden to anyone. Through my teen years, I always had a job, was fortunate to be able to drive myself where I needed to go and use my money to buy the things I wanted. I did not have to rely on other people (except for that whole emotionally needy issue) leading to a strong sense of independence and therefore, control. I learned that if I could take care of myself on the outside and stick with safe, pleasing choices, people would give me the positive feedback I was looking for.

I never gave myself permission to be less than. I have always had a hard time asking for help because I did not want people to think that I couldn't do it on my own. I am strong and independent! Hear me roar! Yet, I was constantly scared of letting people down. But now, I own that part of me, and I have shifted the way I feel about control. Now I know that control is toxic. It's my very need for control and that "comfort zone" mentality that has contributed to my physical and mental health. One hundred percent. There's a better way to live.

It must have been around 2nd grade, after my millionth doctor's appointment with some specialist or another. Both my parents were seated at the kitchen table my mom's little townhouse in Worthington, Ohio. As a child of divorce, this is a crystal-clear sign that you are entering a serious conversation. I'm sure many of you are familiar with the whole "family meeting" scenario. Typically, the meeting is not announcing some great Disney vacation or new inheritance coming your way. At the same time, I knew I wasn't in trouble because I wasn't in to breaking rules. No way. I was already well on my way to making safe, smart choices. I clearly remember being told that I had Rheumatoid Arthritis as if I was being given a death sentence. (Now, I had actually been diagnosed at three, but what's the point of explaining that to a toddler?) As I was getting more involved with sports and other activities, my parents felt it was time to fill me in. I didn't really understand the issue with this diagnosis. I remember thinking that some kids had seasonal allergies or asthma and a boy in my class was diabetic. Ah, the innocence of being eight. I smiled, maybe out of confusion, when my parents told me I would not be able to be as physically active as other kids. Specifically, I asked about dance and cheerleading (could I be any more of a safe stereotype?). I was told "no," those activities would not be possible for me. Hmmm.

Well that's a heavy load to take in on a Sunday. Not acceptable. That was not going to be me. I made the decision, quietly to myself of course, that this disease would neither define me nor determine how my life would play out. I would make that call, not Rheumatoid Arthritis. Perhaps this was the first time I dared to defy anything or anyone. I went on to dance 4-6 days a week including all genres from lyrical, modern and traditional ballet until I graduated from high school. I may have lost a few toe nails along the way, but I also earned the role of Cinderella and other solos at the Palace Theatre downtown. I collected bruises through years of both cheerleading and lacrosse in middle and high school. RA did not define me, although it did make the struggle harder and my determination more intense. After countless injections, blood tests, knee drainings, medication changes, and heath scares I am still defying this disease. I'm just much better prepared.

Good Morning, God.

Or Is It Good God, Morning?

Writing about my Grandmom Servick has been my biggest challenge yet because there is just SO much to say and so many stories. She had a large role in raising me since we lived in the same town and she was often the go-to for sick and snow days. Grandmom, like the rest of my family, had a great way of teaching perspective. The jokes, stories and one-liners always had your belly laughing and heart bursting. Even as a young mother, if her girls were having a bad day she would say, "You'll feel better if you curl your hair." Meaning, brush it off, lift your chin and get on with it. Here is another one of her classics.

"Two sisters wake up one morning. One bows before her bed, folds her hands and says, 'Good Morning, God.' She continues to thank Him for all of his blessings. In the bed next to her, her sister struggles to open her eyes with the morning sun peeking through the blinds. She dramatically throws her delicate arm over her porcelain face and sighs 'Good God, morning!'"

Everyone has a different approach to life. The glass is half full or half empty. Live each day like it's your last, versus plan carefully for the future. Even within the same family and upbringing, people can have dramatic differences in how they live their life. I witnessed this vast difference throughout my childhood between my Grandmom and her sister, Great Aunt Sallie.

Grandmom was vibrant and fairly carefree while going about her day. She made time for friends, cups of tea, the Clinique Bonus sale, Macy's and Johnny Carson. Meanwhile, her sister, my Great Aunt Sallie, was an actual nun in Brooklyn, New York. When I say nun, I don't mean that she acted saintly, so we just referred to her as a "nun," although she did. Aunt Sallie was a legitimate, ordained nun who spent her days teaching in Brooklyn. I mean, come on. It seems fictional and far-fetched, but this is part of the hysterical balance of my childhood.

My Aunt Sallie made frequent visits to Ohio throughout the year and was always a staple part of the family dynamic. She would meet up with us each summer at whichever beach house my Grandmom had rented out for all the aunts, uncles and cousins. The two of them could not be more different, and often bickered like an old married couple. My Grandfather had passed away years before, so Grandmom and Aunt Sallie were just two peas in a pod. By "pod," I mean a pod of sugar and spice. You love them both and they go together well.

Any of my 12 cousins could clearly recall one evening sitting around the kitchen table in Hilton Head, as we often did after family dinner. We would linger around; waiting to hear what game or activity Grandmom had planned for that evening. This is what we do. We eat together- all of us, no matter what size the condo, house or hotel room. We pile on chairs, couches, stools, and floors, anywhere our people are: we gather. First, we eat, then we play. Family vacation is no time to be alone. It's not an option, and because we are kind of unique, maybe even strange, no one wants to be alone. I'm pretty sure all Servick family members suffer from FOMO (fear of missing out). So, we linger, and linger until Grandmom tells us what we will be doing and how much we will love it. Because we WILL love it, or at least pretend we do. She's always right even if we try to fight it, so everyone participates.

This particular night, Grandmom was in the mood for jokes. In her usual style, she waited until she had captured everyone's attention, which was a natural talent anyway. You know those people who will just kind of look at you and you're not sure if you are in trouble, or if they are admiring you? She had that kind of power, and she had you, like it or not.

With all our curious, adoring eyes on her (because we did adore her), she shared this joke. "There was a young man with two heads. He was on his way home from work and decided to stop off for a drink. He walked into a bar, took off his hat and set in on the bar. After ordering a drink and making small talk with the bartender, he finished his drink and went home. When he got home, he realized that he had forgotten his hat. He walked back into the bar and said, 'you may not remember me, but…"

And that's it. That's the joke. That's also the point when my classy, sassy and sophisticated Grandmom fell apart.

She could barely get the ending out because she was hysterically hyperventilating on her own words. Finding the punch line too hysterical to even get out in one breath. We're talking the kind of laughing when you're on the verge of spitting and snorting. Tears rolling down her face, and shaky hand over her mouth in a way that we thought there must be more.

But there was no more. The ending punchline is "You may not remember me." Right this minute; you are either laughing hysterically, which means you are equally as insanely witty as my Grandmom. (If so, congrats. That's an accomplishment!) Or, you are confused, like most of us were. Huh?

Grandmom went on to explain, as the tears and short, rapid, breaths continued. "How could you NOT remember him? He had TWO HEADS! TWO HEADS! Of course, the bartender would remember him. Who wouldn't remember someone with TWO HEADS?"

Ok. That's pretty good, Grandmom.

But that's not the part of the joke that made the rest of us lose our minds. You see, my dear Great Aunt Sallie was aghast. Shocked. Her face mirrored the look of someone who just witnessed a disgraceful act. A crime, a tragic accident, or maybe a catastrophic natural disaster. This reaction coming from a lady born, raised and teaching in the heart of Brooklyn, NY. She absolutely was offended by the joke, no question about it.

My dear, sweet, kind, Great Aunt Sallie felt that Grandmom was mocking people with disabilities. You know, all those people walking around with two heads? You've seen them, right? Every day, they are just walking around with their two heads. Apparently, Grandmom had offended those people and their families. Lord, help us all. Obviously, this was not Grandmom's intention.

Yes, we tried explaining to Aunt Sallie that there are not people with two heads, generally speaking, but the damage had been done. And this only put my Grandmom, and the rest of us, over the edge of insane laughter. Some jokes cannot be justified. So, you laugh. And laugh. And laugh.

In that moment, and so many others, time is frozen. It's like on TV, when they want to show how important a heart-felt scene is to the viewer. You know how they slow it down? I think back on that time, and it's a slow-motion camera panning on each face, hand and tear. It's captured and its mine.

Thank goodness we have Great Aunt Sallie on our side in the end. Goodness knows the rest of us will need her pulling for us when the time comes.

There are the "Good Morning, God" thinkers and the "Good God, Morning" people. People who see the light-hearted humor in a joke, and those who worry about offending others.

Here's what I know: You need both.

You need to see and feel life both ways. The Yin and Yang, the good and the bad, the brutal and the beauty. Grandmom and Great Aunt Sallie.
In the end, we need each other to help us see that.

Count Your Successes

Count them like sheep.

As human beings, we often make lists in our heads of everything we did wrong that day. How many times have you laid in your bed going through all your woulda, coulda, shoulda's?

I was too rough on my kids. I should not have snapped at my spouse. I could have handled that situation differently. Did my kids eat fruit today? I really need to reinforce the importance of teeth brushing. Oh crap, we are in charge of soccer snacks. The list goes on…

Maybe you live in a perfect universe where you feel good all the time about every mistake-free choice that you make. If that is the case, I am pretty sure that we cannot be friends. You may be lovely and all things wonderful, but we will have to part ways so that I don't self-destruct in the midst of your perfection.

Why don't we ever fall asleep listing all of the things we did well that day? There's sure to be more than a few, right? Please say "yes." We are so damn critical of ourselves and the ones we love. Seriously, what is wrong with us? I tell my kids to compliment others and make them feel good; yet focus on my own mistakes? That's messed up!

Thinking back to my childhood in the 80s, I have very few negative memories, minus my fashion choices. (I did, however, have the perfect hair for that generation. I could rock the "mall bangs" like nobody's business. Ask anyone in my 6th grade class. Pretty ironic now.) This was not because negative things did not happen, though!

I am a product of the "D" word. (Shh…divorce.) I know it's that nasty "D" word that people have to whisper and are timid to throw around. As if they will catch it! Like it is a synonym for failure. I assure you that divorce happens to loving, supportive, family-oriented people with the BEST of intentions. HELLO, I am right here as proof!

My parents could likely tell you all of the "mistakes" they made while co-parenting my brother and me. They probably spent many nights listing all of the things they could have done differently.

But here's my memory: Love. Love. Love

I cannot list one example of a time one parent spoke negatively of the other. There was not one significant event in my life that BOTH parents were not present for: recitals, sporting events, and parent-teacher conferences. We even powered through awkward family meetings until I was in college. They were constant examples of LOVE and SUPPORT.

Do you think they fell asleep at night thinking, "Let me list all the things I did right today? Wow, I really killed it in the parenting department." No way. And I kind of think that's crap. Don't they deserve to feel good about making so many of the right choices? Don't we all?

Think more of your successes, less about your mistakes. Your life and people in it are just too damn good to think otherwise! The mistakes will always be there. Always. But, so will the good stuff. Don't get swallowed in the woulda, coulda, shoulda's. Fall asleep thinking of the successes! So, start listing yours.

Pride of the Dung Beetle

I have been compared to many things in my life, but never a Dung Beetle. Until now.

Each year, my cousins and I have a themed gift exchange. We try to steer away from typical ideas and have done themes including, As Seen on TV, thrift-store, quote inspired, Ghost of Christmas past/present/future, hand crafted, etc. No matter what the theme, the gifts never disappoint. There are countless group texts filled with brainstorms all of which are filled with out-of-the-box, slightly inappropriate ideas that I am not comfortable sharing.

This past year we went with "What is your Spirit Animal? "Each person needed to identify the Spirit Animal, come up with an inspired gift and give an explanation for the cousin that he/she was assigned. As you may have guessed, this could go many directions. Some chose to actually research Spirit Animals and be honest and loving, others wanted to have fun with it and then there's the cousins who went with cruel and insulting. All of which generally take place during the cousin gift exchange. You know to expect the unexpected.

To explain the choice of spirit animal, you can expect to hear rhyming couplets, haiku poetry or a quick Google search at the time of gift reveal. Creativity and laughter are a GIVEN. It is often ridiculous and completely out of hand. All of the craziness is a direct reflection of our grandmother who taught us to laugh at ourselves and each other, and to wrap it up with a rhyme.

A very kind, big-hearted cousin had selected my name. I was ready to get teary eyed over a comparison to an eagle, lioness or some brave, beautiful animal. Definitely something bold yet sentimental. Ha! That was not what I got. Once again, I should have known to expect the unexpected. When I pulled a hand size, glittery beetle creature out the gift bag...surprised was an understatement. Another cousin yelled out "That's a DUNG BEETLE!" and I was all, "No... that would be ridiculous." After all, what do I have in common with a bug of any kind? I mean, gross. A bug that eats THAT. What is the comparison there? Apparently, this cousin went with cruel and insulting.

And then I read the description on www.dictionary.com.

" A DUNG BEETLE IS NOT ONLY THE WORLD'S STRONGEST INSECT BUT ALSO THE STRONGEST ANIMAL ON THE PLANET COMPARED TO BODY WEIGHT. THEY CAN PULL 1,141 TIMES THEIR OWN BODY WEIGHT. THIS IS THE EQUIVALENT OF AN AVERAGE PERSON PULLING SIX DOUBLE-DECKER BUSES FULL OF PEOPLE. "

Enter: glossy eyed heart melting.

I understood what she was saying. She was both admiring and reminding me that I was strong. Maybe even the STRONGEST. She knew the year I had. The hardest year yet. A year filled with piles of dung around every corner. You've all had years like that, or at least days or weeks. She knew I had to choose how to deal with the challenges that 2016 so generously delivered. She thought I met the year with STRENGTH. I was able to deliver 1,141 times my strength. Just like a Dung Beetle. **Bam!**

I am overwhelmingly honored to be a Dung Beetle. (And relieved it was covered in sparkly glitter.) Inevitably, there will be dung to deal with in the future. No doubt. Hoping you find your inner Dung Beetle and deal with it with strength.

The Gatekeeper

I thought I was "Worldly," but it turns out I'm just "Mid-Westernly."

Have you ever started over in life? I mean completely started over? The kind of starting over that involves leaving your family, friends and only city you've ever called home. Walking away from a family that involves four sets of parents, aunts, uncles, cousins and friends you've had forever. Where Sunday dinner can involve anywhere from 6-30 people and monthly dinners with friends you've known since 7th grade still occur. I promise this is not my life according to the Hallmark Channel, this was just my life. Safe, secure and predictable. Just like me.

When the opportunity for my husband to expand his career on the West Coast came up, it was unexpected. Being raised in Columbus, Ohio, we have never pictured ourselves moving further than North Carolina or Illinois. We had a happy, foreseeable life surrounded by an immeasurable support system. However, life is about "dreaming big" and we wanted to show our young children the importance of taking the adventure. So, we made the six-day drive from Columbus, Ohio to Anaheim Hills, CA. (That's a whole other story right there! If you're considering a road trip with two small kids and a dog- do it. It will forever be one of my favorite memories.)

Years ago, my dad gave me a copy of a speech my Grandmom had written called "From Brooklyn to Buckeye." It describes a time when my Grandfather, their four small children and herself moved to the Midwest. She considered it the "ultimate adjustment" in her life. Wow. I get it now.

I've been to Spain, Portugal, Caribbean Islands, Mexico, Brazil and all over Ireland. I'd met people from all over the world, love culture and have an open mind about life. I'm sure I will find "my people" in sunny, Southern California! They all seem so nice!

In my Grandmom's speech is the story of the Gatekeeper. This is a story that my Grandfather used as an example when they made the move to the Buckeye state.

"When travelers arrived in a certain city and asked the Gatekeeper what kind of people lived there, he asked them what type of people lived in the town they had just left. If they told him the people were warm and friendly, he would tell them that the same kind of people lived in this town. If they told him the people were cold and hostile, he told them that's the kind of people they would find here."

Sweet. I knew loving, kind, open, honest, amazing people in Ohio. Therefore, that's what I will find. Whatever Grandmom says is truth! I came to Orange County open, honest and ready to put myself out there. You will find the people you were looking for.

That was my first mistake. Poor, naive me.

I assumed everyone else was open and honest. However, it turns out, that may not be the case here where it's always sunny and 78 degrees. UGH. Damn Midwestern roots! These Ohio values and morals will break your heart. Are we friends? Are we not friends? Where are my people?! For a sunny state, there is SO much grey! Seriously, Gatekeeper. What gives? So, I did what my Grandmom would have done, I kept looking. And guess what? It may have taken 9 months, but I'm finding the honest, kind, real, open-minded people. MY people! People like you.

Don't get me wrong, in my first 6 months, I met a solid 5-6 people that I knew I could trust and trusted me in return. (If you're reading this then you are one of them!) And in the last 2-3 months I've really been able to connect with the same type of friends and family I left behind in Ohio.

The Gatekeeper was right. You find what you are looking for.

Look for the good. Look for honesty and kindness in others. But keep in mind that you may have to be patient. Take your time. I no longer consider myself "worldly," but I take great pride in my Ohio roots. As for my naive, trusting, Midwestern morals, I think I'll keep them!

Grandmas Run the World

You know what's the BEST thing in the world? The thing that might "save" all of us? Better than deep-fried anything, sandy toes or even a dry, oaky glass of wine?

Grandmas.

Yup. Grandmas.

I'd venture to bet that if your grandma ran for president right now, you'd vote for her. If not, you'd vote for one of mine. Not only would the Oval Office be filled with beautiful Belleek china, and Irish lace, there would also be the aura of empathetic, witty, stubborn Irish women. (Not to mention some kick-ass theme parties where people come dressed as their favorite Johnny Carson guest.)

I realized this week that my determination to constantly push through pain, stress and medical experiments has little to do with me. I am both cursed and privileged to be riddled with the genetics of headstrong, determined, hilarious women.

Grandmas run the world.

One of these ladies took a spill this week severely breaking her nose. Do you know what she wanted before surgery? Aspirin! Because she's that hard core. That badass.

At 87, she takes zero medication and goes for walks every day. No wonder I don't have it in me to back down. She's not a drinker either. A few years back, she mowed the lawn because that's what grandmas do (see what I mean?). A neighbor offered her some lemonade. She thought it was strange it was in a bottle but found it delightfully refreshing downing it a little too quickly. Feeling a rush of energy, she began mowing all of the neighbors' lawns. Can you imagine? The sweet little Irish lady down the street, mowing the whole neighborhood after one Mike's Hard Lemonade? I just love my family tree. Because of Grandmas.

Luckily, my other Grandmom cultured me in the pleasures of a good glass of wine, or the occasional airplane mini-liquor bottle. Equally important life skills. Because of Grandmas.

It's also why some of us may sing or hum simple directions to our kids like "please go put on your shoes" or "She's my girl... ".

You can't tame their spirit.
You can't boss them around.
You can NEVER count them out.

But...

You can rely on their love in your ugliest times.
You can feel their laughter in your fingertips.
You can slowly breathe them in and hold them in your heart even when they are gone. Trust me on that one.

We are all better people because of grandmas. I'm not saying my grandmas are better than yours, maybe I am. We can all agree that grandmas are pretty damn incredible.

It Turns Out You CAN Go Home Again

Relationships are complicated. People are complicated. It's not the complicated part that separates people. It's the silence. The unwillingness. The lack of effort. Obviously, there are exceptions here considering I am nothing close to a relationship expert.

(Disclaimer: There are times when the "complicated" is nothing short of a tangled-up spider web and should be left alone. Or, because some people are just crazy! You all know somebody. No judgment here. Just stating the obvious.)

When I chose to move and leave my people, I knew it would change my relationships. I wasn't sure how, but I knew things would shift in one way or another. I was worried that when I returned home, I would feel different and less connected. However, I drastically underestimated the heroic combination of my family, friends and technology.

DRASTICALLY. You guys, cell phones save lives when used wisely.

As it turns out, the distance meant NOTHING. (Well, it meant SOMETHING, like no more free babysitting, but you get the idea.) I, without a doubt, owe the success of my relationships to technology. I am not sure if I owe the creators of all things iPhone a personal Christmas card, my life savings, or what. If Facetime asked for my first-born child, I would have a hard time declining the request. Of course, it's about choice and making the time as well. My family chose not to be silent. Not to let the distance weaken our relationship. We were all willing to put in the effort to not only maintain but strengthen our bonds.

It's easier to be silent. Easier to sit back and let time pass by as you wonder why people aren't calling YOU. I've learned that I am no victim. I make choices. I make an effort.

Because of the LACK of silence, it turns out that I can go home again. Can you? Make the call, send that email or text, put in the effort. It may surprise you.

"When You're Homesick, You're Sick"~ Roberta Servick

I actually stole this line from my Grandmom after she moved from Brooklyn, NY to Columbus, Ohio with their four small children. Until I made such a drastic move myself, I didn't realize that homesickness leads to heartache. And heartache, my friends, leads to actual physical symptoms.

If your heart is not happy, it often results in depleting health. Since moving to California, my RA symptoms have been at an all-time high. Although there are outside factors that contribute to my RA, the fact that my heart is in Ohio is equally significant. I've had to dig deep and look for my "Reset Buttons". I could have let it all swallow me up. I was close to drowning in self-pity, with every glass looking half-empty. Then one afternoon I found that speech written my Grandmom in July of 1979.

Writing. She chose to write. She chose to use her "Reset Buttons" by getting involved in things that made her happy. When feeling lost or empty people need to reset!

So, I went for my personal "Reset Buttons":

- Nature- so, it turns out California is pretty beautiful. By "pretty," it's actually GLORIOUSLY beautiful. I mean, have you been here? Going for a walk or a simple look out the window can recharge my happy thoughts.

- Ice water or carbonated water with a slice of lime IN a wine glass – a few sips later and I am left feeling refreshed, healthy and fancy! (It's important for me to feel fancy when I am wearing my yoga pants and sorting little socks.)

- Family Escape- another shocking fact here…California has a TON of magical, adventurous activities for the family. We can drive 20 minutes or a few hours and discover places people don't see in their whole life. Pack a picnic and hit the beach, or a hiking trail. This is our go-to plan when we are missing a family party back home. (Ohio is still referred to as "home.")

- Family Texts- This is my #1. I likely drive my siblings, parents, aunts, and uncles and cousins NUTS with my rapid and rampant texting. When I feel myself slipping or swimming I pick up my phone. I send them my writing; I send stupid memes and emojis like a twelve-year-old who just got her first cell phone. It settles my heart, as obnoxious as it may be.

Lesson I learned here? I know how to reset myself and I often need resetting when dealing with pain and being homesick. The trick? USE your "Reset Buttons!" What are your "Reset Buttons" when you need a pick-me-up?

For Goodness Sake, Let Them Love You

Nope, not quoting a Justin Bieber song. That would be "Let Me Love You." Plus, not much of a Biebs fan here. Nothing against him, just not really living in a pro-Bieber state of mind. And I'm not going to apologize for it. Maybe it's because I own a mini-van now.

And if I know ANY of the lyrics, it's because the radio LOVES it some JB. Damn, those catchy little beats! How do they stick in my brain? You may or may not catch me humming the tune or whispering the lyrics under my breath. Promise. Not a fan.

When I started posting my medical journey for others to read, I did NOT want to attract sympathy or pity. I started it because once I began sharing, I received such incredible support and understanding from others with autoimmune frustrations. My goal was to connect with those going through their own journey AND create a format for those who support us and want to understand us.

However, every time I post, I receive virtual hugs, kisses, prayers and general well-wishes. To be honest, at first, I was like, "No, that's not what I am looking for! Stop with the 'oh, you poor thing' garbage."

I took all the POSITIVE VIBES as sympathy. I felt pitied and weak. I was frustrated that people were feeling sorry for me. I kept asking myself- why are you making this public, then? Why put it out there? Why do people keep sending their pity?

Then, my mind cleared up and I thought, get the heck OVER yourself! These people don't feel sorry for you. They are not pitying you! They LOVE you.

THIS is how they show love. The "hugs," "likes" and motivating, positive messages are exactly how people show love. This army of friends and family NEED to "give" their love to me, as much as I need to receive it.

So, let them love you. Let them text you fist-bump and muscle flexing emojis. I can be strong, brave and resilient and STILL accept prayers. I can be a fighter and STILL allow others to lend compassion. I can be VULNERABLE and POWERFUL at the same time. It is meant to add to my strength, NOT make room for weakness.

If your loved ones are sending similar messages your way. LET THEM! **Let them love you.** Lucky you and lucky me. We need each other.

It's What We Do

We do family.

How many of you grew up with your cousins as your favorite friends? And your aunts and uncles as your guardians of fun? A great benefit of moving back from California is that we are only hours from our family and friends around Ohio. Now that we live in the same state as most of our family, we are able to do the family festivities. We spent the weekend traveling to Columbus and Cincinnati to fit in four birthday celebrations in 48 hours. This is our idea of fun.

People generally react with much less enthusiasm than my family when it comes to booking our schedule. "Ugh- that's a lot of family time!" True. But as for my reaction: Lucky me. Lucky us that we have so many people that want to see us and include us in their most important days. And they want to be a part of ours. Lucky us to fill up our weekends making stops to laugh, play, eat and drink with some of our very favorite people. No time to be lonely. No time to feel sad.

Tired? Heck yeah.

Low on patience? Sure!

Stuffed? You bet.

But above all- Lucky.

And now I get to watch my God given friends raise their own little people. Witnessing them as (mostly) responsible adults, doing responsible things. However, with one single glance to any of my cousins, we are taken back 10-20 years. Transformed to the days of Nutcracker battles, dressing up in Grandmom's nightgowns, Black Friday shopping, and scavenger hunts. She was the architect who designed the blueprint for our indescribable, unbreakable and occasionally dysfunctional foundation.

She taught us that when it comes to family you:
Show Up,
Speak Up,

And Dress Up (in costume if needed, which it generally was).

Do I miss the California sunshine, 70-degree weather, mountains and palm trees? Well, yeah! You're crazy if you don't. It really is an amazing way to wake up each day. Would we trade all of that (literally all of that because Cleveland does not have ANY of those things!) to be able to be a part of four birthdays in 48 hours?

Hell yeah. Any stinking day. We did and we would do it again. (Except in February, I really miss sunshine in February.) But other than that, call me crazy. Call me family obsessed. But, also- call me happy.

Marriage Glamping

I don't know about you, but my marriage is a lot like "Glamping". You know, glamorous camping.

I'm estimating that a good 40-60% of my marriage has been spent living the dream in renovated homes. By renovated, I mean we live in a home that's half construction site, half beautiful. Within these nearly 14 years, it's safe to say that 30% of our magical memories were created without a fully functioning kitchen.

To our credit, we have cooked family meals while accommodating the various stages of remodeling. In our 20s, we cooked two months of dinners (mostly mac and cheese) on the grill. This was throughout January and February thank you very much. While living in California, we went another three months without ANY kitchen appliances (except a fridge) and mastered life with a combination of grill and microwave meals. (And that's ONLY talking about kitchen renos!)

Let me be honest- if your marriage can survive multiple home remodels, your chances of beating the divorce rate is in your favor. We've cooked with visitors, living with little kids, and bearing the elements of seasons. (This was not an issue in Southern California where we could BBQ every day. They don't call it "cooking out," for you Midwesterners.)

And yet, we do it AGAIN and AGAIN.

Through the fighting and frustration, we CHOOSE homes that are kind of ugly, or outdated. Partially because we are cheap, but mostly because we get a thrill out of drawing up our own vision and making it come to life. We love throwing ideas off of each other and it has been worth it every time. Or, at least it's worth it when it's over.

Which brings me to our current situation. I LOVE our home, and...

- I don't mind that we have not had countertops for a month (you would think I would know someone!).

- I can handle tripping over the tools, shopvac and air compressor.

- I don't even mind turning my laundry room into a coffee station.

- All the good I've done to help the environment is rapidly going out with the trash as I consume paper products for every meal.

- I've become accustomed to my garbage can on TOP of the cabinets so that the dog won't get in it.

HOWEVER- this week I have lost my beloved garbage disposal and kitchen sink. You guys. Moment of silence. It's not a big deal to get a drink from the laundry room sink or do the dishes there. Here's what I am struggling with: It's Thanksgiving.

While making pumpkin pies for the kindergarten feast, and chili for the piano potluck, I am taking some time to mourn my garbage disposal. How many times do you think you use yours? My estimate, 1,000,000 times a day. I can't rinse chili meat down the laundry room sink and my house now smells like ground chuck.

Yes, it's temporary. Typically for us, though, one week quickly turns into one month. and so, it goes. On the bright side, the convenience of grabbing what I need from the top drawers is astonishing thanks to the lack of countertops. I haven't had to open a draw in weeks! I can literally find gratitude in just about any situation. If not gratitude, then a whole lot of humor. One thing I know about any situation I am in, good or bad, "this too shall pass." Even if it passes like a kidney stone.

Life Is a Bike Ride

(Here's the story behind that one. A glimpse of how my family works.)

Do you remember what it was like to ride a bike as a kid? Can you close your eyes and go back to that free-falling, anything is possible, feeling? Can you remember being excited, scared and free all at the same time? If you're unable to connect to that inner child freedom- ride a bike right now. I'm serious. Whatever your age or athletic ability, try riding a bike. I bet it's not all that different.

Recently my dad and his siblings (all somewhere in their 60s) took a trip to Kiawah Island. (Side note- my parents 60s is NOT our grandparents 60s, am I right?) They took full advantage of late-night card games, good food, a few casual swear words, but mostly there was a lot of general good old-fashioned family fun. If you have ever been to Kiawah Island, South Carolina, you would know that it is mainly a biking and golf town. It is slow, beachy and laid back, pretty much the opposite of Myrtle Beach or anything super touristy. It reflects more of a neighborhood feel from the past with spaced out homes and more greenery than a typical beach destination.

The most effective way to get around or head to the beach is by two wheels. While all my aunts and uncles are healthy, successful real-life grown-ups (because to them we will always be the kids) they are not regular peloton cyclists. So, for a few of my favorite people, hopping on that bike was like being a kid. I was not there, but I can imagine the laughter that took place within the first few minutes. I couldn't even begin to grasp the amount of sarcasm that occurred while mounting the bike. I can actually picture one aunt in particular, literally holding on to the handle bars, shaking in attempt to restrain her laughter.

If you know my family then you already understand that my dad and his siblings grew up in Brooklyn, New York where people show support differently than in the Midwest. I am very aware that I inherited my sarcasm, whit, and snarky tone from these very people. And I thank God for it every day. While my family is dedicated to the church and God is always at the center of our celebrations, you are not likely to hear "Hop on, sweetie. You can do it. Just believe in yourself." Ha, not a chance. For the record, my Grandmom HATED the word sweetie with a passion as strong as her faith. Chances are, it would have gone more like this, "Come on. Get on the bike already. You do realize, every one of your grandchildren look better on a bike than you, right? Don't be a wuss."

You've got to be tough in this family. We don't mess around. But we do laugh, a lot. One of my cousins sent out a meme that said, "What if I end up marrying someone who didn't grow up being roasted every second of their life and I have to watch what I say?" No, thank you. That pretty much sums up how my cousins and I were raised. At the same time, I bet you one million trillion dollars not one of us would trade our childhood for a thing. I would double down on that bet if you asked any one of us if we felt loved. We are raising our kids and living our lives with every ounce of that love. I know many of you can relate.

So, these love-filled, goofy 60-somethings rode those damn bikes around every day of that trip. When I called my dad to ask about the trip, he got very serious which is rare, so I knew to pay attention. I pulled into the Giant Eagle parking lot that Monday and grabbed my journal (because you never know when an idea might knock you over). My dad and step-mom are very comfortable on bikes, partly because they love Kiawah, and partly because they refuse to grow old. My dad wanted me to know the advice he gave his siblings. I was listening.

"Look at where you want to go. Not the distractions. Don't look at the beach, or the marsh or the people that might get in your way. If you want to go left, look left. If you want to go straight, then you need to look straight. And then, you need to go."

He went on to say that they used that as their metaphor for the weekend. It was so simple, and he knew I would analyze the heck out of it. He even joked, because he knows me well, that this will end up in one of my posts one day. (He refers to this as "going viral.") But who can blame me? I mean, this is GOLD! Life IS like riding a bike, isn't it?

You guys, it's this easy:
Decide where you want to go- with work, relationships, personal fitness. What's your goal? What do you want?
Focus on where you want to go- keep that goal in mind every day.

Don't be distracted- keep that focus, don't worry about the sidelines because the distractions WILL always be there.

Yes, it started as a simple bike riding lesson for baby boomers, but it is EVERYTHING every generation needs to be hearing, doing, sharing and modeling. So, what do you want your life to look like? For me, it's finding the next steps for my writing and sharing my message which is actually incredibly frightening to put down in ink.

How can you focus on that goal to make it happen? For me it's a lot of researching on publishing. As John O'Leary states in his book <u>On Fire,</u> *"Whatever you focus on, in life, grows".*

Keep the focus! I can't be distracted by my other responsibilities or nay-sayers. If it is really important for you to get to that destination, you have to make a plan, not an excuse. You have to stay focused

Get on your metaphorical bikes, focus on where you want to go, and get your ride on. Ready, set, go!

The Opportunity

It wasn't unusual for me to make a Target run after seeing my arthritis doc. Whether in California or Ohio, something about Target can lift a girl's spirits after being poked, prodded and patiently waiting to see one technician after another. Target is very much a universal love language. It's one of the few stores that has its own memes and coffee mugs written about it. One spouse loves it, the other hates it, right? That's the joke anyway. It is factually relevant in my home, so the joke makes me smile.

It also is not usual for me to check in with my parents and catch them up on my progress or lack thereof, depending on the day. I'm sure I've mentioned that my dad also has rheumatoid arthritis, so we like to compare meds, opinions and notes after our appointments. Although my dad did not develop RA until his 30s, his genetic history definitely contributed to mine. You could say, as I often do, that my dad gave me arthritis. But it would be unfair to only give him credit for that trait without also giving him credit for my sarcasm, whit, thick skin, and positive perspective. So, yeah, I blame him for the damn RA. But I also give him full credit for the good stuff. And I'm pretty proud of the good stuff. Overall, I'm still in the "winning" column.

Pulling in to a ridiculously small parking space, as typically found in Southern California, my dad listened to my excellent visit with my new rheumatologist. We laughed at the fact that we were now on the same medication and both felt good about where I was headed. Chatted about the beautiful weather in Anaheim Hills, and winter in Columbus, Ohio. The usual family update on the kids and husband. You know the drill. The conversation quieted a bit as it often does toward the end and I began to turn off my Cherokee to head inside for a little retail therapy. (But if you ask my husband, we NEEDED that throw pillow!) Before I hung-up my dad said something along the lines of, "while I've got you on the phone, let me tell you about my new opportunity."

Assuming it had something to do with work or volunteering, maybe even one of his snowmobiling boys trips he does once a year, I kept listening. However, then he let on that his heart doctor had given him an opportunity. Hmm. An opportunity? What kind of opportunity could that even mean? At this point, I was completely confused and told him so.

He replied, "I have an opportunity to increase the blood flow to my heart."

I kid you not. Word for word. If I close my eyes, I can still hear him saying this. To me, as to most people, this did not seem like a positive opportunity. In fact, it sounded downright terrifying. Once again, I told him to explain what he meant. He, matter-of-factly, as if giving me the grocery list, described his heart and that there was blockage in one of the tube things. (This is where I get a little fuzzy trying to digest the details.) I know he mentioned the aorta and something about chambers maybe? There may have been valves and atriums, but the part I do remember is needing open heart, quadruple bypass surgery. And that was really all I could take in sitting in a crowded Target parking lot, even on the sunniest of days in beautiful Southern California. There could have been a hail storm and I would have missed it. (But I would have said "Oh, Hail No". Because it's funny every time.)

Mostly, I was really mad about it. Like, angry, somebody-better-explain-this, mad. At that time, and for many years, my dad lived a healthy, active lifestyle. He didn't drink alcohol or caffeine. He rarely indulged in chocolate or unhealthy meals. He made his health a priority for years. He was doing everything right, and still. STILL? This is where I metaphorically throw my hands in the air. The genetics handed to him included a complicated heart. And that was that. It wasn't fair. It wasn't deserved. But there we were. As my dad once said, "So, now what?"

Now what? Now comes the silver lining. The place where we choose to focus our attention. The stress test he had done that day is what discovered the blockage. Had he not had that test on that day, we may not have found it until after a heart attack. Good news. Him being in the medical industry allows him to identify the best docs in their specialty. Good news. My dear friend who is a nurse anesthetist in that same hospital was able to refer us to the best in that field. Good news. My husband and I were able to figure out how I could get home and be with my family. More good news. My family. My dear sweet family. We are force of prayer, support and sarcasm. We've got each other. Armed with snacks, hugs and laughter. Always. The best news.

But the part of all of this that matters most is not the blockage, not the struggle and not even the support or the silver linings. It's the way he chose to look at this challenge. He had an "opportunity" to improve his health. And to him, that was a good thing. That was the space where we would live. As a family, we turned this challenge into an opportunity. An opportunity to grow stronger, love deeper, and be even more grateful. That one liner which my family are so good at, has changed how I look at my challenges. "I have an opportunity." What a great way to see the world. Your life. Everything.

After a successful surgery, my brother, sisters, stepmom and I went to visit him. And although he may not have been looking his best, he was able to slip out "The other kid got hit by a bus." He was half-conscious, hooked up to machines and loopy. However, he was able to think back on our family story of perspective. I knew what it meant- things could always be worse. At least I'm here. I'm still standing. (Or, laying, but you get the picture.)

Years later, my dad is doing great. Still living a healthy, active lifestyle. More quinoa, less steak. He would say he has an opportunity to eat quinoa and salmon where others would complain and moan about it. Usually once a week or so, there's a family text about someone's opportunity. Sometimes it's serious, but more often it's a little silly and snarky. Like me.

In the midst of even the darkest challenges, your most difficult days will give you countless opportunities. The rest is up to you.

Chapter Two: Surprise! You're Not Perfect. Can We All Get Over It Now?

Let Your Life Smack You in the Face

Stop taking the things for granted!

Can we just talk about the idea of "perfection" for a hot second? If you are working toward this image of perfection, whether it's your job, children, marriage, or your body- NEWS FLASH: It will never happen. It's total bullshit. If you do think you find it, it is not for long, because as soon as you think you obtain this "perfect" thing of yours, the real-world steps in and all of a sudden, your "perfect" slides into the "not good enough" category.

If you can't tell, this fires me up.

Look at your life. As it is. Look at it right now. It's good, bad and full of imperfection. Am I right? Chances are your imperfection is someone else's GOLD MINE. Did you miss the memo that there is no such thing as perfect? Nobody has a perfect life.

Yes. I know it's easy to get caught up in the "It will all be so good if I just had_____, or I just looked like _____." We can all do that until the freaking end of time! What a way to live, constantly striving for the next best thing. Never really sitting where you are and appreciating it. What type of message does that give the world about you? Telling your friends and family that you and your life is not good enough because people will pick up on that, big or little. The feelings of inadequacy will trickle down.

Personally, growing up in an "imperfect life," according to society at least, and having struggles forced me to take off my rose-colored glasses at an early age. I did not have the luxury of taking my family, health or marriage for granted. They've been dangled in front of me like a carrot, leaving me to choose between fight and flight. It's in that process that I honestly stopped caring that much about the materialistic bullshit.

More than anything, I've learned to like me. Yes. I just wrote that. I like me, and I worry less about people who may not. I've learned to appreciate the things my body can do and less about what it can't. It is strong and has continually gotten me through 100% of my challenges proving to me that we are so much stronger than we think. But we don't stop and think about the amazing things our bodies have done for us. We take it for granted and focus on our weaknesses.

There are no quick fixes about life. I have mentally and physically put in the work. Everyday. I have to continue to put in the work. No excuses. It's not easy, but it's a choice I make.

I could focus on my imperfections; Lord knows I have plenty of them.
- *Growing up in a divorced family. (Like over half of the U.S. population!)*
- *Putting my back-to-school clothes on layaway…at Kmart.*
- *Dealing with the physical set-backs of Rheumatoid Arthritis since the age of 3. Countless injections, fluid drains, med changes.*
- *The effects of these meds which have taken a toll on. My body and will continue to do so.*
- *Countless terrifying moments awaiting test results from early mammograms, lung biopsies, scopes, blood tests to rule out scarier terminal diseases.*
- *The insecurity of losing my hair, having it come back, and knowing that at any point in time it could all fall out again, for the rest of my life.*
- *Visits with rheumatologists, pulmonologists, endocrinologists, GI specialists, dermatologists and some I'm probably forgetting.*
- *Others that I keep private.*

How many of these "imperfections" do you live with? How many times have you left the doctor hoping for the best, but consumed by the fear of the worst? How many times have you physically not been able to dress yourself? Maybe you've moved back and forth to your mom and dad's houses for your adolescent years? I'm not pointing this out for sympathy. I'm totally at peace with my struggles and challenges. (Which have become opportunities.) I'm pointing this out for a little perspective reality kick in the arse! Because if you've had struggles, I mean down on your knees desperately praying for strengths kind of challenges, you know what I mean. And I bet you see life differently now. How many of those days have you survived? Every single one of them. And I do NOT take that for granted. I refuse.

Look at your life! Don't take your life or your struggle for granted. Stop striving for some unobtainable image of perfection and look at the gifts right in front of you. Let your life smack you in the face a little bit! Enough already.

Dance in the Rain

Yes, me. The person who craves control and routine. The same person who usually discourages mud and mess. I actually encouraged it.

My gut reaction was to yell, STOP! Command them to grab an umbrella or get inside! Go in your safe, warm, cozy house like the rest of the neighborhood! But something brought my brain to an abrupt halt. Like someone turned on a light in a dark room. Huh? What was that?

Do you ever have moments like that? When you're headed in one direction and then it's as if someone shakes your shoulders saying, "No, not that way. THIS way!" Hold the damn phone. Do I really want safe, cozy kids going out into the world? Or do I want little humans who embrace the rain. Kids who get OUT and live life? I don't want kids who are afraid of getting wet (not talking about literal rain here, folks). I want adventure seekers!

Why am I trying so hard to control the situation? (And likely most situations in my life if you ask my family.) What do I get out of that control? Who wins from my kids going back in the house with their heads down knowing they were right on the verge of the best day ever? Nothing. Nada.

You guys, you should have seen their little round faces. First glance was wide-eyed concern that they were in trouble. So, as my son told my little lady to stand under the tree as he grabbed the skinny branch above her- I approvingly smiled back. You've seen pure joy on a child, right? That look when they are juuuuust about to get away with something? It was like I handed them a non-verbal permission slip to the magical land of childhood. I mean, the saying "Life isn't about waiting for the storm to pass, it's about learning to dance in the rain," isn't just a cliché (although I'm not a big fan of clichés). It's for real. Here I am navigating my way through a hell of a storm and my kids are like, "Hey, MOM. LOOK! IT'S RAINING! WE SHOULD DANCE!" We should celebrate it!

The giggling, wide-eyed wonder was in full effect. For that few minutes, while they took turns shaking branches on each other, the rain falling all around, they were a team. Brother and sister tied together with strands of raindrops and laughter. I may have stayed safe and cozy under my umbrella, because, well, baby steps are my style, and this "letting go" business takes work.

Let it go.
Let it be.
Let them be little.
Dance in the rain.
You get the picture.

New Rules

I've made some new rules for myself since the "Falling Out" began. (I realize the term "Falling Out" is a bit dramatic, but this is how my brain works.) My only new rule is to make LESS rules.

Like many of you, I've always given myself unspoken rules or guidelines on how to live my life and I tend to be incredibly disciplined about them. I'm assuming this is what many people do, or maybe I'm the only weirdo who likes all the pillows perfectly arranged on the couch before I can go to bed with a peaceful mind. From what I eat, how much I exercise, cook, keep a well-kept home, etc. You get the picture. Annoying, I know.

Now before you accuse me of being a Stepford Wife, I created these rules for my health and well-being. Rules that fit my life and goals, (but, here is what I learned), AT THAT TIME! But life throws curveballs that shift your thinking. Making disciplined rules for yourself is an effective way to achieve your goals, right? But what about when your goals change? What about when the floor falls out from under you? Your health, divorce, family hardships, or simply being unhappy can do that to a person.

No one lives an honest life without the floor dropping. No one. Whether it drops slow like an elevator, or fast like a roller coaster, floors always drop. When looking at my life I realized that my self-made rules no longer fit my goals. Before the "Falling Out," my headspace was relatively clear, and my mind was mostly calm. But it was like I was living my life according to CliffsNotes rather than really reading the book. (Are those even still a thing?) When I read a book, I highlight, make notes and think about it. If I do that with a book, why am I NOT doing that with my life? Geez. Am I even listening to myself?

New Rules:
1. Wake up first and sit. Usually outside, with coffee and a book. Without

technology. Sometimes reading. Sometimes writing. Sometimes literally staring at the squirrels and birds in the yard.

2. Stop all the planning. The meals, the kids schedule, the pillow organization. Enough already.

3. Go easy on myself. The gym, ice cream, parenting, all of it.

Live less disciplined. Take more slow, deep breaths. Chill the hell out.

Not one person in my life expects me to be perfect. Nada one. So, chill the hell out. As my goals continue to change throughout my life, so will my rules. (All current and future rules will include, French fries, ice cream, wine and writing. FYI.) No more missing out on the fun and living by CliffsNotes. I'm messing up the throw pillows and doing all of the good things.

Don't Be Moved

"As for me, I shall not be moved" ~ Maya Angelou (Grandmother's)

It's taken me some time and a whole lot of life experience to understand what Maya Angelou was talking about in this poem, specifically in this quote. In fact, it took a whole chapter of Brené Brown's book, "Braving the Wilderness" to create my own interpretation. You see, it's all about being who you are. Standing tall and proud and unwilling to be moved. Seems simple, right? But, if you're not sure who you are then you shall be moved all the damn time. Most of us are a little messy and all over the place.

We are constantly being pulled in one million and three different directions. Volunteer for this, sign-up for that, all while creating Pinterest-worthy parties. We are so very busy being the unrealistic image social media demands us to be. Often compromising our values or priorities to go with the crowd. Sometimes it's much easier to please the masses and keep your mouth shut than stand up for something. No one wants to stand out. And heaven forbid we make a fuss!

Lay low.
Blend in.
Play it cool.
Go with the flow.
And my favorite, sit there and look pretty. (Insert gag!)

But what if that "flow" isn't what you want? What if your compliance isn't fulfilling your heart? What if going with the flow does not make you happy? Thank goodness for my challenges and obstacles because they have given me the opportunity to firmly plant my feet. I'm learning who I am, what matters most and what I stand for. Health issues, relationships, big moves and parenthood. They are hard. They are deep. They are real life. And they can sure as hell move you.

So, "plant your damn feet. Bend and stretch and grow. But stay true to who you are," Brené Brown. My feet remained easily planted this summer when it was easy to push aside responsibility. But as fall and schedules pick up, it's so comfortable to slide back into old ways. The volunteering, the judgement, the hectic routine families face along with scheduling cute coordinated family photos in time for holiday cards. It's exhausting and unauthentic.

During that time, my overwhelming breath was thick enough to fog up a mirror and my feet began to slip. The heavy guilt of needing to be everything to everyone can force you to move. Rather than letting my feelings get the best of me and moving my feet, I reminded myself- I shall not be moved. The pressures and struggles may force me to bend and stretch- but I shall not be moved. I know who I am. What's important to me. Time for myself. Time for my family and friends. The things that make me happy. Those very things will NOT be uprooted. Lay that Catholic guilt on heavy because I'm not going anywhere. My priorities will remain in place, and I will say "no" as needed. I don't have to do it all. I don't have to be everything to everyone. The world will keep right on spinning. I just have to be everything to myself. "As for me, I shall not be moved."

Stand tall.
Plant your feet.
Play it your way.
Be the flow.
Don't be moved.

Be Everything to Yourself

One day I decided to swing. By myself in my backyard.

A random thought popped in my head the other day: What if I stopped trying to be everything to everyone else? What if I started trying to be everything to myself? What's the worst that could happen? Yes, I know I have responsibilities like feeding my children and keeping them alive and occasionally bathed. There are bills to be paid, checks to write and obligations to fulfill. I am an adult with all those adulty like things we are required to do. I get it.

I had a sudden urge to go outside on a warm, dry, July day. The sun was out as blue skies peeked through the quiet, still trees. Our 1980's playground swings caught my attention in the back corner of the yard. (I kid you not, the previous home owners left their steel pole set with two swings.) What if I just felt like swinging instead of folding laundry? No one will die, right? The house will not crumble. So, I squeezed my 38-year-old hips in those little rubber seats and pushed off. Whoosh! Like riding a bike, motor memory kicked in and I began to pump my legs and feel the wind on my mostly bald head. I felt a bit ridiculous and sick, but mostly it was gloriously freeing just like when I was seven. This was much more exhilarating than folding socks together. How could I have let myself forget about this feeling? Have you forgotten? After eight or nine pumps my daughter came outside (after screaming all around the house because she could not find me for like, seven seconds) and stopped in shock at the sight of her mother swinging.

"MOM! WHAT ARE YOU DOING?" she exclaimed with the biggest smile.

"I felt like swinging! Is that weird?" Said this giggling mama.

"Nope, you're just a grown woman on a swing, I guess," replied the sweet girl.

Calmly stated like it was no big thing. As if it was a usual occurrence in our house. I guarantee you; it was not. She didn't even care, or notice, that I was not doing "adult" like behaviors. She thought it was hilarious and delightful, and maybe even a little surprising. She saw me enjoying the moment without any judgement of it being strange or weird. How do you think your kids or family members would react if they busted you swinging your heart out?

No one even cared that I was being everything to myself for a bit, and not being everything to them. They actually thought it was refreshing. Mind you, after staring at the blue sky with the hint of the brightest green tree tops sneaking in, I had to sit up REAL slow. I mean, SLOW MOTION speed. Even then, the world a hazy cluster of shapes and colors. I was more than slightly dizzy and nauseous. Nothing like a few minutes on a swing to make you feel like an adult.

Climbing on that swing is NOT like me, but I'm going with my gut (nauseous or not) and living my life. Being there for others is an AMAZING thing! And the world needs people to help people.

But if you're busy being everything to everyone else? Who's busy being everything for you?

'Tis the Season

After talking with some brilliant, open-hearted, best of the best kind of friends and family, I'm reminded that the world's priorities are a HOT MESS! To those of you willing to admit your imperfections- Halle-stinking-lujah!

Please, please, be imperfect. Perfectly imperfect. Put it out there. Let others find comfort and strength in themselves as a result of your openness. Because they will, I promise they will. Even people you least expect it. In fact, those are often the people who need to hear it the most. They need permission to NOT be perfect. Give it to them. Let that $hi! Go.

Over the holiday, be thankful and all of that happy, jolly business, but more than that LISTEN to each other. Really listen. The kind of listening when your eyes don't wander around the room. Where you're not thinking about what you need to pick up from Target on your way home, or that email you need to send to the teacher. Focus on what people are willing and wanting to share with you. They may have chosen to talk with you because you matter to them. Don't jump in with a comparison of your own life, at least not at the beginning. Let them finish with your full attention. This is something I have really had to purposely work on. I'm a horrible interrupter! I feel the need to show interest and empathy by bringing my story into the equation. Guilty. It is done out of the best of intentions, but it's rude and it changes the focus of the conversation. I bet I have missed out on some great perspective or connections with people because my need to share has overshadowed them. I'm regretful of that to the point where I get a stomach ache if I think about it too much. I hate that feeling which is why I continue to remind myself to be a better listener each day.

While conversing with these important people, ask questions you want to know the answers to. Mean them. Be authentic. If you don't want to know, don't ask and then ignore their answer. I can't tell you the number of times I was beginning to answer someone's question only to see them literally look distractedly past me. Don't we all know the difference anyway? Obviously, there are times when you are just making small talk and are naturally less concerned with the answer. But wouldn't be amazing if we all put in the effort? Wouldn't it be great if we at least tried to mean what we say, say what we mean and give each other the attention we deserve? Obviously, it's not possible 100% of the time, but it's not that hard to put in the effort when the person or conversation needs it.

These are your people. Listen to and validate them. Show them the real you and give them permission to do the same. We all are a bit of a mess anyway! So, let's celebrate that for once. I'd like a lot less of the, "Oh, everything is amazing. My kids are just such a blessing. Have you seen my new pair of shoes?" Rumor has it I'm not the only one getting tired of this false reality.

Puh-lease. Come. On.

We all love our kids, family and friends. Every stinking one of us. It's not a contest where you win a free t-shirt with "I love my kids the most!" printed on it. No one is listening to you saying, "Oh, I wish I loved my kids as much as Cindy." Nothing to prove here. If you can't be you, then let that stuff go. If there's one thing I've learned, it's that the people you need most will love you anyway as your authentic, sarcastic self.

After all- 'Tis the season.

Celebrate the Stubborn!

Some days you wake up ready to take on any challenge in your way. It's the cliché commercial when a beautiful lady with perfectly placed hair and fresh-faced skin stretches one arm into the air while gracefully pulling the crisp, white sheets off the bed all while smiling to herself. Let's Do This! Bring It On! Watch Out World! Just like the rest of us, right?

I'll admit, there are days when I wake up with this mindset, although not necessarily the same grace and even skin-tone. I may wake up optimistic, but it is with the stench of morning breath, bird-nest style of bed head, a bit of goop stuck in my left eye and possibly a damp pillow. And then there are days like today. Our senior citizen dog has little control over her body functions and pooped on the floor, again. My kids are still suffering from the Halloween Hangover and have likely been taken over by sugar-filled maniacs. My son lost his shoes, which I can't begin to wrap my head around. I remembered it is "share day" for BOTH kids. Who am I to prevent them from feeling special at school today? Because it's just so important that we keep reminding the younger generation of their uniqueness. (I'm assuming you've caught on to my sarcasm there.) And my husband was packing for his trip to Vegas for a few days. All before 7:45 am.

Throw me a STINKIN' bone here! Honestly. There is no fresh-faced mama greeting the day while inhaling dog poop and annoyingly argumentative little people. Not today, friends. We will need to set the "Take on the World" attitude on the back burner for now. Put aside the optimistic, glass half-full outlook. No "Positive Vibes" approach to my day. Sometimes it's all about survival and you just do the next necessary thing. One ridiculous responsibility at a time.

Today, I am going with STUBBORN. And coffee. A few cups of coffee and seven sprinkles of stubbornness will be my survival tools. I often hear, "How do you keep such a positive attitude?" or "I wouldn't even know you are dealing with Rheumatoid Arthritis." Yeah, well let's just take a moment and give a shout out to my Irish heritage! Cheers to my fellow stubborn people! You may not know who you are due to the fact that you are likely too stubborn to admit that you are stubborn, but I see you. I admire the way to keep your head down, no complaining and just take care of business. Much love to you! Slainté!

When you don't have the strength to be all sunshine and rainbows about life, you can rely on this skill. A persistent approach to NOT giving in and letting the daily stresses of life get you down should be CELEBRATED. It has gotten me through physical pain and mentally tough times. Yes, when battling my children over candy, or playing card games, stubbornness has its negatives. I HATE to lose and often insist on doing EVERYTHING by myself just to prove that I can. However, today I am going to Celebrate the Stubborn!

Disclaimer – My husband may, at times, disagree with the level of stubbornness I am able to achieve. He will celebrate it 64.5% of the time.

Run Like Phoebe

With the idea of "perfection" around every corner, I decided to dive in a little deeper. How do I view it? How do I apply it to my life and the people around me? I've spent a lot of time and put in a lot of work evaluating my idea of perfection. But in that process, I've dismissed the perfection I expect from the people around me especially when it comes to my little family. While overcoming my perception of this imaginary goal, I've wasted too much time expecting it from my family. Apparently, they cannot read my mind, which is disappointing, therefore they don't know my expectations. No one in my house is perfect and that's okay. What I realize now, is that striving for perfection is actually unhealthy. Like, toxically unhealthy.

Brené Brown describes perfection as "Teaching them to value what other people think over what they think or how they feel. It is teaching them to perform, please and prove."

Read that again. Is that what you want your children and loved ones to do? Perform, please and prove? Gross. Pretty sure that's what I spent my first 35 years doing. I grew up needing to please parents, teachers and friends, which left very little time to figure out what really made me happy. I mostly found happiness is making other people proud. The desire to make your loved ones happy is not an unhealthy trait. The world needs all of us to look out for each other, however, it can't be the sole motivation for how you live your life. Due to my past, there's a good chance I'm unconsciously putting that expectation on my children. The vicious cycle of imperfection continues.

According to society's expectations of little girls, my sweet thing does not fit in the box. In all honesty, neither of my kids fit in that box and thank God for that! My daughter's idea of matching is wearing one flower pattern on her pants and a flashier flower pattern on her shirt, or maybe polka dots. She probably also has on two different color socks, inside out of course because of the weird toe texture thing, and cowboy or camouflage mud boots. This girl wears what she is feeling without any regard for expectation. Cat leggings with a pumpkin shirt, hell yeah! Whatever. So, coordinating colors is not a God given talent. That's fine. Even though she's well beyond her toddler years, she is an emotional dresser. Meaning, she wears what makes her happy and comfortable. It's been a difficult quality to swallow as a mother who craves control. Painful, at times. Walking into a social function, I have to fight the urge to defend my parenting by letting people know that I let her choose her clothes. It's wasn't me! I swear! There are days when my husband and I have turned our heads away hiding a cringe-worthy or goofy smile, but we've agreed to let her be who she wants to be. That's just the way it's going to be for her. Accept it.

One time at an exciting 1st grade volleyball match. Any of you who have been to a 1st grade volleyball game know that by "exciting" I mean, praying for the serve to go over and another child to at least pretend they are going for the ball, missing contact on the high-five, and gymnastics on the court, As my sweet, feisty girl was running to the back of the line, another mother lovingly asked if I ever saw the episode of "Friends" where Rachel and Phoebe go running in Central Park. Spending my teenage years in the 90s included wearing flannel shirts, boot-cut jeans and knowing every episode of "Friends." Leaving those of us in our late 30s-early 40s to recite any line, like "PIVOT," at the drop of a hat. I know many of you are laughing about that truth and maybe wanting to binge watch it tonight.

Now, it's important to know that this mother is one of those people who whole-heartedly loves all children as her own. She was not teasing me about my girl. In fact, she was celebrating her individuality the way many of us grew up accepting and loving Phoebe. My daughter runs with her whole body. Arms, legs, fingertips, elbows and smile. Completely uninhabited by the way it "should" look when you run. You can actually see her whole, free spirit beaming through her movement. If you can't picture it, check YouTube for this episode.

And I let it go, you guys. I just let it go. Like her clothing choice, I had to let her own it. Without shame or finger pointing. For one thing, I want her to live in this happy place with the fairies as long as possible because it won't be long before peer and self judgement steps it's ugly cowboy boots in her life. No matter what your struggle has been, if you are reading this, you know the reality I am referring to. I'll be damned if I will play the role that makes her think she is not enough. Yes,

I'm more comfortable sending a well-groomed, coordinated little lady into the world. Or, perhaps maybe one with slightly less flailing. Just maybe.

But, and I mean a big but, (my kids would think that line is hysterical by the way), not if my little comments or sideways looks make her feel less than, or that something is wrong with her. Because once that starts, then comes the shame. And that shame will change who you are supposed to be. Like a storm cloud on a sunny day, it can change everything. It is not hard to recall a time in my life when shame stepped in. I can easily close my eyes and remember the feeling in my gut when someone asked, "Why does your nose look like that?" That flush feeling of heat in my face and wanting to hide in my room and never go to school again. You know what? She's never going to be perfect. I'm never going to be perfect. And more shocking news, you're never going to be perfect either. Looking and playing the part of perfection does not build confident, self-assured big girls.

It can be really hard to ease off or drop those perfectionistic urges and habits. But maybe we can just agree to loosen our stance on them a bit. Can we agree to do that? For the children? Realistically, pumping the breaks on perfection and letting people be who they are is good for all of us. Essential, in fact. Because whether it's how you talk to others, or what they witness from your actions- it affects them more than you think. So, at some point this week, run down the hallway or out in the parking lot and flail your hands and legs. Feel the weight of perfection as it beams out of your body. For goodness sake, go run like Phoebe!

Choices Are Better Than Excuses

I'm tired. There are bills to pay. There're not enough hours in the day. My kids are the worst behaved children ever. My family won't eat healthy foods. I'm just not happy with myself. The list goes on and on.

We all have excuses, but guess what? We also have choices.

You know what's more powerful than excuses? You guessed it, choices.

Life is hard, guys. But it's just not that hard to live it well. You've got to make the choice. Don't make that harder than it needs to be. Try not to complicate that fact. Keep it simple. Make a decision right now. What do you want your life to look like?

Before you get all judgy and "oh, there's goes Angie on her high horse again with her fancy wig and annoying positivity". Let me remind you, I have excuses. I've got plenty of them. (Side note – not a pity party. Just a reminder that life is a battlefield baby and I'm fighting the fight just like everyone else.)

For example:
- *Diagnosed at age 3 with Rheumatoid Arthritis*
- *Sat down around 3rd grade and told I would NEVER get to participate in physical activity. At my kitchen table. By my parents.*
- *Product of divorce at 3 years old. I will never know what it's like to grow up in a duel parent home. Don't think that doesn't affect somebody. It does.*
- *Spent my childhood desperately trying to be the perfect kid and make up for everyone else's imperfections and to hide my own.*
- *Never feeling like a totally fit in.*
- *Brother diagnosed with AA and losing all of his hair his 4th grade year, my 2nd. (Goes back to trying to be "perfect".)*
- *Subsequently losing my hair at age 38.*
- *Infertility struggles*

- *Countless medical anomalies- countless injections, nodules on my legs, nodules in my lungs, lung biopsies, infusions, cracked ribs, x-rays, CT scans, scopes in personal places, and that's just off the top of my head.*
- *Moving across the country and back in support of family and adventure.*
- *Medications starting with baby aspirin at age 3 and a list too long to divulge without putting you to sleep.*

And YET. Even still, here I am? I mean, come on. I've made the choice to live a life I want to live. And while all of these challenges have molded me, it does not make it easy. You can choose, too. Every day you can choose. You can, you guys! It makes me angry when people make excuses about their health and their way of life. Do you know how fortunate you are to be healthy? Do you know what people would sacrifice to have your health?

I could use any combination of these as an excuse to feel sorry for myself and wallow in self-pity. Right? I could choose to take on that victim mentality like so many do. I can think of a few good reasons there to eat my feelings and binge watch Netflix with my fuzzy Indians blanket and Peanut M&M's.

OR- I could turn these challenges into opportunities.

Because I am a child of divorce, I choose to take my imperfect marriage very seriously.
Because of my medications, I choose to put healthy things in my body.
Because of my alopecia, I choose to be more confident in the person I am.
Because I've had some pretty scary, close call, situations, I choose to live the life I want each day.

I cannot choose the cards I have been dealt but I can sure as hell choose to play the hell out of those cards. So, can you, if you choose to. There are no guarantees in life. You can live and die happy. Or, live and die angry. Let your choices be stronger than your excuses. It's worth it every time.

Call It a Comeback

Have you ever experienced life slowly falling into place? All the little pieces fitting in after all the work and so much struggle. That moment when you start to think, "Holy bananas. This is going to work out. We are going to get there." When each piece of the puzzle has either found a home or is getting closer. There is no such thing as perfect. But I do believe in working for the life you want to live. Putting in the work, the time, the energy, the CHOICE to get where you want to go. Life's a journey, right? Sometimes fast paced sprints, and other times more of a sweat-soaked, blister-on-your-heel kind of marathon. It depends on the day or even the minute.

It's easy to feel positive and hopeful and fulfilled in those moments. They catch your breath and prove good things happen. You've surged through the struggle and now you get to experience the rising. Call it a Phoenix moment if you want. Those are the moments I live for. The highest of highs. When life is in motion and the pain is finally worth the victorious pride that comes with it. These are the days or minutes when you know- ANYTHING is possible.

And just when you are floating on an overflowing fountain of hope with the birds chirping and sunshine in your pocket, the earth shifts under you. You take a second to breathe in positivity but then, bam! In stomps the set-back.

I freaking hate the set-back. I love the idea that the comeback is bigger than the set-back. But, damn. The set-backs are rude, aggressive and no joke. Like ordering your salad without red onion (because I still am not grown-up enough for those) only to find them thinly sliced and diced in a way no fork can escape. Set-backs are not for the soft-hearted. They are grueling, soul searching moments and the older I get, the more treacherous and defeating the set-backs become. It's like picking up your boots in thick mud or quicksand. All that work, all the progress and here you are.

So, what do you do when you are feeling the flow of life one second only to have your life snatched and shaken like a snow globe? Oh look, there goes the laundry flying away in one direction and your sanity in the other. It makes you question your choices, your instincts, the very things that matter most. What do you do with that? (I've tried hiding in the closet with chocolate, and while that works for smaller set-backs, unfortunately it is not an effective method for the big ones. Major bummer because it's really safe and delicious in there.)

For me? I cry, take a lot of deep breaths, cry, pray, talk to people I trust, pray and cry some more. Yes, I realize I've mentioned the crying strategy more than a few times. Mind you, I also cry at every P&G commercial about moms or even The Kids Baking Championship on the Food Network. I require a lot of tears and prayers and deep breathing because I get this tightness in my chest. Like I'm being squeezed by a giant snake, my ribs and lungs taking on the pressure of hundreds of pounds. Fear. Worry. (So much worry.) Literally squeezing the life out of me. That may sound a bit intense and maybe over dramatic, but I am a deeply feeling person so when I'm experiencing a strong emotion, I'm all in. I don't do feelings "Half-ass."

I'll often write private pieces that are just for my eyes and while that's helpful, it's only temporary. I'm still working on the whole "let it go" philosophy. I'm on Elsa's side about this, but it's not always so simple because we don't live in Disney, folks. Although some people insist on believing they do. Those aren't my kind of people. I can generally "let it go" for 3-5 minutes and then I feel the need to analyze and worry.

I've discovered that worrying gets me NOWHERE. Zero progress is made from worrying. Because then I start worrying that my hair will fall out from worrying so much. So, then I worry about worrying! It's so ridiculous. But if you're a worrier than you GET it! (And now I've probably got you worrying about how much you worry. Sorry.) I remember, years ago, there was a story in the news about a man who had killed a family and hid them inside of trees. I can't tell you how many hours I lost looking through my 6 acres of land wondering which trees we would fit in. I realize this is border-line insane and that the chances of this happening are very low. However, it's a perfect example of how my brain loves to twist, over analyze and worry. I was also a new mom at the time, so I like to blame the lack of sleep for my heightened anxiety. Now, I try to focus on ACTION over WORRY and I've gotten better about this over the years. This is an incredibly effective tool often used by my less anxious husband. He's actually taught me a lot about applying it to my life. There are definitely times when action can fix the problem, thus removing the worry. I've gotten hours of my life back by taking action to solve my worries.

I'm worried about getting things done before school- wake up 30 minutes early. I'm worried about getting home from an appointment to get the kids- ask a friend.

I'm worried about eating healthy meals on the table- menu plan on Sunday. I'm worried about my husband's stress level- schedule a night out with his friends or me.

These are easy problems with easy fixes. And I thank God for that. I'm so fortunate for the support system in my life. Grateful for the small worries of my day with easy fixes. I take nothing for granted. But many of my worries, and likely yours, are much bigger than asking a friend to pick up the kids. Right? If only those were our biggest worries.

We all have more serious struggles. These set-backs don't have simple solutions because life is not always simple. Whether it's our health, relationship, employment, or parenting, set-backs can change everything without any warning. So, I can't fix it. I can do everything right. Do life to the BEST of my ability. Follow my instincts, spread love like wildfire, be grateful, and guess what? The set-backs will happen anyway. I don't know all the answers to this one because I'm still working my way through it. It's so thick and heavy and I'm not always sure which way to turn.

> *I have to rely on what I know:*
> *Feel it.*
> *Take a deep breath.*
> *Write it out.*
> *Reach out to my support system.*
> *Say my prayers.*
> *Always be grateful.*
> *Let it be.*

I usually have to cycle through these strategies 834 times a day. But they have gotten me through some desperate, soul searching times before, and they will get me through again. If you don't have a strategy for how to deal with set-backs, you can get lost. You can drown. Suffocate in the intensity of it. Don't do that. Just don't. There is always a "Plan B." In fact, there's a "Plan Z" if needed.

The set-backs will keep coming, I have no doubt. But so will the comebacks.

Chapter Three: Escape the Overrated Comfort Zone

Fear Is Real

O h, my gosh, you guys. I have so much fear. So much fear and doubt inside of me. Enough to end world hunger, create world peace, and maybe even enough fear to fill the gap between the Republicans and Democrats in our beloved government.

It's that deep.

I know I am strong. I know I am brave. Blah blah blah. I have seen dark, ugly days and risen above them. I have felt physical pain, been unable to dress myself or climb down stairs on my own two feet and lived to write about it. I am proud of the struggles I have mustered through because they have made me stronger. The pain has molded me into the person I am. I get it. I've read all the cute quotes that send that message. I've seen the t-shirts with the annoying "Positive Vibes" catch phrases.

But pain, is different than fear. Pushing through fear is SO much heavier for me than pushing through pain. So, what am I so scared of? What are the things that hold me back and keep me up at night? It's so simple. And, yet, cliché as parenting advice. (Enjoy every minute. It goes so fast. PUL-LEASE!)

What if what I put out there is not good enough?
What if I risk it all, expose all of the feelings- and then no one wants to read it?
Or worse, what if they read it and hate it? Even worse than worse, what if they feel sorry for me for believing in myself? I'd die.

The embarrassment of thinking I might actually do it only to be fooled into believing in myself.
What if I disappoint, not only myself, but my whole family?

You guys, I am SO much better at supporting someone ELSE who is looking to take a risk. I'm like the ultimate wing-girl if you are looking to make a change, or newly divorced and want someone to hit the bars with you. I will motivate you, remind you of how amazing you are and do all the encouraging things you need. You feeling up for a leap? I've got your back, but I'm not sure I've got my own. Isn't that depressing?

These are pretty logical fears for anyone who has an inner pull to take a leap. It's called a leap for a reason. There is no room for excuses and absolutely no place for a "comfort zone." (I live so very happily in my comfort zone.) However, I am not an excuse maker- EXCEPT, and it's a really big "except" for a reason. I do not make excuses for my health, my relationships and within my personal life. I do, and with all honesty here, I DO make excuses for not moving forward with my writing.

Here are some of my favorites:
- *Writing is not a "real" job that would actually lead to a career.*
- *Who wants to read what I have to say anyway?*
- *I am not a "real" writer. My only formal training is how to teach writing within grades 4-9. I feel qualified to teach the future of America to put sentences together more than I trust myself. Side note- the 5th graders in this country are probably better writers than I was in college because the stakes are so high these days. So, there's that.*
- *What makes me so special? (Short, deep and the root of the fear for so many of us.)*
- *Why should I get to be so lucky to turn my passion into a career?*
- *Just who do I think I am?*

Right when I think I am growing into my own and finally feeling grounded in my confidence, going with the whole "I shall not be moved" philosophy, I hesitate. I'm working on bending and moving with each breeze, while simultaneously knowing who I am and what matters to me. The one thing that really matters to me is encouraging others to be or become who they want to be! And I want to be a writer, damnit.

(Holy moly, that was just really scary to type into the computer and I may have deleted it a few times before I completed the sentence. Keep writing nauseous or not. Just write the next sentence and then the next, etc.)

So that's it, guys. That's my big, scary dream. I want to write. Write all day with my coffee and write all night with my wine. I want to write about my random thoughts and blurbs and then share them with people who will take that as something meaningful. Through that we can all laugh and feel connected. Because life is so hard and full of disappointed and empty expectations and stupid but necessary detours. But I really want people to know that there is so much beauty hidden in there. And maybe if we stick together, we can find our way through the mud by being grateful for the good stuff while laughing at the ugly straight in the eye. We can do that, right? It's not crazy? Or maybe it is, and I am fooling myself.

But here's what I know to be true:
- *I feel an undeniable pull to get words into the world. And it gets stronger every day. Like a constant voice in my head saying "DOOOOO ITTTT, Angie!" (Similar to the voice in your head from made for TV movies in the early 90s about peer pressure. "One little puff won't hurt you". "Come on, just take a sip. It will be fun".)*
- *I swear to the high heavens, I feel my Grandmom in the room. And she's loving it. It's an overwhelming, tears in my eyes, tight chest feeling. So strong, that I often talk out LOUD to her while I write.*
- *The "Why NOT me?" voices are getting louder than the "Why me?" voices. I hear them through the books I read and the people in my life. The voices of John O'Leary, Jen Hatmaker, Glennon Doyle Melton, Rachel Hollis, Maya Angelou and Brené Brown. I hear the encouragement from the actual people in my life (not just in books) who tell me I have to put it out there. Just write the book and worry about the rest later.*

To be honest, I don't know where this will lead me. I do know I want to keep writing and sharing. I don't know what the next steps are, my target audience, or how to move forward. But I am ready to find out. I am ready to do the next right thing. Even if that "right" thing is the hardest thing I've done. My bones are telling me that it's time. I'm going to follow the experts and listen to my inner voice. Serve the work. Don't stress the final product or the big picture. Focus on the words and tell the story. Less "why me" and more "why not me?". Lift your chin, Angie. Do the next right thing.

Be That Girl

In the wake of the world and all of its' ugliness, there are so many battles to fight. Many of us are looking for the glimpses of glory. (Is "glimpses" even a word?) Here is a suggestion: Be that girl. Be that guy. Be that person.

There are very few things I am experienced in: sarcasm, various arthritis medications, and being the new mom. I can tell you that anxiously fidgeting at the school pick-up line is just as uncomfortable in your 30s as it was in my teens.

Whether it's at soccer practice, parent night, dance lessons- you guys know the mom I am talking about. The one that likely lingers a little too long even though the kids are ready to go. The parent that smiles at you as she walks to the car, quickly making eye contact. The one trying not to butt-in your conversation but wanting so desperately to be a part of them. Chances are, she's slightly intimidated and incredibly overwhelmed. She's me. And maybe, she's you, too.

I know it's comfortable and easy to stick to your routine. In your busy life, it's so much easier to walk away and go about your day with your tribe and your own lovable people. "Not that there's anything wrong with that!" (Please excuse the cheesy Seinfeld reference.) But if you're looking to spread a little kindness. If you feel the need to add a little goodness to the globe- talk to her. Ask her to coffee, wine, a play date. Just. Ask. There is nothing to lose and we live in a world where we need to take more risks to make people feel included.

Be that girl. Be that guy. Smile and ask.

After all, I'm just a girl standing in front of other moms, asking them to love her. (Can you name that cheesy movie reference?) Make the world a little kinder. One lonely mom at a time.

Show Up. Repeat

No matter what type of pain you are dealing with, we all want a quick fix. Take this pill. Do this exercise. Start eating quinoa and kale. Do a magic spell. Whatever. There is no quick fix for pain. Even a paper cut hurts like hell for a few days.

Show up and face the pain anyway.

I've discovered parenting is not so different. I have expectations for my children. Clear, simple, 'be happy and kind' type of expectations. As if it's just so easy to raise good children who will positively contribute to society. But there is no straight line in parenting. Just like with pain. I am a jumbled, squiggly line type of mom. Like many of you the distance from point A to point B is a hot mess of loop-de-loops rather than a smooth, even glide.

One of my children spent 20 minutes trying to convince me that parent-teacher conferences had been canceled. This child went on to explain that a letter would be coming home with details the following week. Did I mention this child is a 1st grader? Yeah, sure kiddo. The same said child gets a color-coded behavior chart each day, just like the other students. One particular day, the chart did not reflect my motherly expected color. (Ok, it was more than one day, but I'm doing my best here!) My little love went on to tell me that it was "free choice color day" and they got to choose ANY color they wanted! It didn't mean they had a rough day. Um hmm. Right.

Luckily, after 12 years teaching Middle School, my child didn't stand a chance. I knew this game well. I had enough run-ins with student shenanigans to prepare me for days like this. This isn't my first rodeo little buddy. (Let me just take a second and say "you're welcome" for contributing such greatness into society.)

Parenting does not go according to expectations.
Show up anyway.
Pain does not go according to expectations.
Show up anyway.
Life certainly does not go according to expectations.
You got it now, show up anyway.

(Friendly reminder, this is a judgement FREE parenting zone. However, prayers are always accepted. Lots and lots of prayers. We've got a long way to go.)

Less Planning More Living

Stop planning and live your life. Honest to goodness.

The best choices I've made, I didn't see coming.

I've always been a planner. A bit anxious. Needing to know where we're going, what time, who will be there, what I should wear. Craving the expected. Safety. Willing to live my best life- as long as it was in my comfort zone. I would have assumed that I'd teach 5th grade forever. Live in Columbus forever. Same friends. Same little circle. Happy, but predictable.

I would NOT have guessed, I'd be writing this from the comfort of my Cleveland home, sipping apple cider vinegar, with handfuls of hair next to me in the trash. I would NEVER have imagined being a stay-at-home mom, celebrating one-year post-California adventure, attempting to warm up my stubborn arthritic fingers. The expression "life throws you curve balls" is an understatement. More like, "life throws you curve balls, which are also on fire and spitting daggers as they zing through the air." That's more accurate.

But....

Let me repeat what I wrote at the beginning - The best choices I've made, I didn't see coming. Because while I could not have predicted the struggles, I also (and much more powerfully) could not have predicted the joy. I could not have predicted the calmness of a deep breath. The support of good friends. The endless comfort of a spouse. The surprising snuggles of an eight-year-old boy. Or, that I would learn to talk less and listen more.

I would have never guessed I would love my body more at thirty-eight than twenty-eight. I would judge less and accept more. That dancing in the kitchen with your little girl is soul soothing. Or, that I would be licensed to MARRY people! I most definitely never would have planned to pick up and move to California and learn to always say "yes" to the adventure. Accepting another adventure by heading on to Cleveland. This is NOT "comfort zone" living! None of this was in my plan. We have been down, unemployed, scared, uncertain, but always willing the take the risk. Choosing to see that risk as adventure.

Important thought here: Because we are up for any adventure, we are also up for any challenge. Big challenges like my health, moving or employment. As well as small challenges, like choosing where to go to dinner. (Which can sometimes be a big challenge, too!)

Focus on the living, not the planning. Surprises are often the best part of life.

Chances are, your vision won't go as planned anyway. Always take the adventure.

Yes. Yes, You Can

Still feeling the love of recent birthday wishes! If there is one thing I've learned (hopefully more than one), it's to GO FOR IT.

Risk it.
Jump it.
Have faith and hold on tight.

I grew up more of a baby steps, "play it safe" kind of girl. But something is happening as I creep up on 40. I gain a little bit of "who the heck cares?" and lose a little "but that's not the rule!". I pictured my life as a teacher, mom and wife, growing old in the same city with all eight of my parents and siblings. As many of you know, life LOVES to throw out those tricky curve balls. It brings you unexpected challenges and even more surprising opportunities. People and circumstances push you beyond your comfort zone and you have a choice to make. Feel sorry for yourself and be a victim or grab life and choose joy.

When faced with these challenges, I keep coming back to this: What do I have to lose?
- My friends? Nope.
- My family? Nope.
- My health? That's already a hot mess, so I just have to let that one be.

In the last few years, I've made the choice to walk away from a career I loved, fought ridiculous health battles, moved across the country and back again, struggled to be the mom my kids need me to be and tested new personal professions. Each choice left me more understanding of who I am and who I want to be as well as mentally/physically stronger. The end result is a level of happiness I had not yet found.

They say you find your true self as you get older. I'm not sure I'm there yet considering I still struggle to come up with a dinner menu and probably watch too much Bravo. But you are more willing to get out of that comfort zone, don't you think? For me, I see things differently now. It's like your brain shifts in to a victor rather than victim role. This is thirty-eight. Sure, I'm collecting wrinkles and an uneven skin tone. And somehow when I look down, I see hands that resemble those of my grandmother's. Thirty-eight will bring more frequent trips to the salon for grey coverage. All of this is happening. Ready or not.

However, my age also oozes a quiet confidence and peace just knowing that I really can do whatever the hell I want in life. So, I'm going to. And you should, too. The things that matter most will still be there. You can live outside of your comfort zone. Yes. Yes, you can. Not everyone is so lucky to get this choice.

Push It Real Good

If you are thinking of making a big change, and you are worried, like SO worried about how other people will react- do it anyway. I promise it will be worth it. It will be scary and hard and give you all the jittery feelings in your belly. And you will doubt yourself and second guess everything. I mean, everything and everyone. But if your gut, your instinct, is still pulling you in that direction? Listen to it. You guys, your gut instinct is SO underestimated. There is a reason God, or science gave us those intense feelings. It's not by coincidence. They are not to be ignored. So, if you are looking for that push, nudge, or maybe a giant SHOVE. Here it is. I can gently encourage you with my words, or I can come hunt you down and physically shove you if need be. I am little, but considerably strong for my size. Seriously. I can be a tough girl if you need me to be. Tell me where to find you and I will be your personal shover. If you live far away, I require room and board and possibly a glass of wine. But I am quick witted and fairly entertaining.

Once you do it. Oh, man. Hallelujah.

Those of you who have taken a leap know what I mean, right? It's difficult to put into words because the feeling is that powerful. Once you follow your instinct and truly listen to what is it you want (because we all know finding what you want is often the hardest part,) it's like a freaking Disney movie. I'm not kidding. The people you were worried about will shower you will their love and support. They will flock after you like wilderness animals from Cinderella. The birds will sing for you, the mice will coddle you and deer will bring you your clothes in the morning. Okay, maybe not all of that. But STILL. The people will show up in masses. It might NOT be the people you were expecting. And some of the people you were worried about might need a minute to wrap your head around it. But be patient with them the way you were patient with yourself. You didn't get to this point over night either. Give them time.

When I styled my half-grown alopecia hair as a pixie- I was sick about it. Sleepless. Hesitant. All of those things. I wanted to hide in my security ball cap forever, even though I kind of hated that, too. But when I showed up at the salon, it was like I was prepared for battle. Convinced, in my gut, I was doing the right thing. Even if it was the scary, right thing. Because often that is the same thing.

Since then, random strangers who do not know about my hair situation have poured their compliments on me like syrup. Thick and heavy with kindness. Oozing over me like a heated blanket. My kids, though? Totally freaked out about it. My daughter tried to hide her little quivering lip and looked away the day I showed up without a hat at school pick-up. Once I went in for the hug, she fell apart because it did not look like her mama. I gave her time and space. Let her adjust to the newness of my look. Do you know what she said while I was cooking dinner later that night? She walked right up to me chopping carrots in the kitchen and said, "Mama, you're beautiful. It's different. But you're beautiful." See what I mean? Freaking Disney stuff right there. We can make the hard choices and do the scary things. We just have to trust ourselves!

So, consider yourself "pushed" out of your happy little comfort zone. Get on with the show, guys. You get this one life to do the things. Now, get to it.

Woke Up Happy Today

Not sure if it was because the sun is out, my bed is a slice of heaven, or because the dog slept through my Mindful Break. As I looked over some comments from my recent social media posts, there may have been a bit of deep exhaling going on. Sometimes people are too much. Not like too much wine, or too many potato chips that leave me feeling not-so-great in the end. More like having too much blue sky or too many sunsets. No. Such. Thing.

There are many reasons I do write. (NONE of which include pity, or sympathy. Coddling makes me feel weak and sad.) I write for me.

- To clear my headspace (it's really foggy up there sometimes and I don't always know which way is up).

- To feel a little bit lighter. You know, get it on paper and let it go? Let it go, Angie, let it go.

- To release any anger, this is also to the benefit of my family and society for that matter. No one wants an angry, bitter mom at the grocery store while on summer break with her charming kiddos all day. So, you're welcome. It's really a community service!

There's absolutely NO doubt that the supportive, touching and witty (often my favorite) comments make my life better. But truth be told, everyone NEEDS to be told these things! So today, yes TODAY, tell someone else. Tell a stranger. Tell a loved one. Someone old or someone young. Tell them they are a rock star, that you are inspired by them, that you notice them.

It WILL be uncomfortable.
It WILL be awkward.
It WILL take you out of your comfort zone.

But, not much overwhelming joy come from your comfort zone. Tell them anyway and watch their reaction. It's magic I'm telling ya. What I love most about words is the power to choose them. To put them in a way that shows people that life IS, in fact, hard. So, what? Each of you reading this (if I've kept your attention this long,) is struggling with the heavy, ugly side of life in some way big or small.

You see, we can't wait for the perfect circumstances to join the party. It's time to wake up and participate now. Because every moment matters. Every day counts. Every minute is an opportunity.

I hope you see that my story is a testament that no matter what adversity comes your way, it's not the end of the story. If you can learn to see it as an opportunity to overcome, to learn, to stretch, to wake up, to ask, where might this be leading me? – you'll realize the strength you have within. And it's more than enough. ~John O'Leary

---

Life is hard. So, what? There are no "perfect circumstances". So, what? As the excerpt from "On Fire," by John O'Leary explains; participate, because it matters.

I suggest reading the excerpt a few times over. It's a good one. Now, go be uncomfortable and awkward today and watch the result.

Live for the Overture

Have you ever been to the theatre? Not the movie theatre, or even a small outdoor production. But some sort of theatrical production, Broadway or not, requiring an actual curtain. The kind of curtain that's thick, heavy and maybe even tide with a braided, gold rope. Likely, you were sitting on red velvet chairs that flipped up and down when you stood up. The kind of theatre that you have to stand to let people through because the seats are packed in like sardines. When you look up there's probably intricate gold paint outlining an age-old mural in warm burgundy tones. And every time you wonder how someone was physically able to complete such a painting. Then to each side, you admire the mini balconies assuming they were put there for regal use and curious as to why they are now only used for big, fancy lights. The kind of show you would get dressed up for, maybe even have a special dinner on the town before you find your seats. Can you picture it now?

I remember my early years at the theatre like it was yesterday. My Grandmom Servick was BIG on theatrical productions. Having grown up in Brooklyn, New York she developed her love of all things dramatic and made it a part of her children, and eventually grandchildren's life. If she wasn't taking us to the theatre, she was turning the family home into one. We've reenacted the Nutcracker, Wizard of Oz, Johnny Carson Show, Saturday Night Live, and countless family scripted scenes. Too many to count. And as much as those Grandmom Theatre productions are at the center of my childhood happy place, there is nothing like the theatre.

Do you want to know my favorite part? It doesn't really matter. I'm assuming since you are reading this that you want to know me. Whatever. It's not the stand-out star with the voice of an angel, the big finish that leaves you in tears, or even the encore.

You know that moment right before the curtain goes up? That matter of seconds when the lights dim, and the crowd begins to hush? With one deep inhale, you turn toward the stage, eyes fixed on that velvet curtain. In that pause, engulfed in the silence and darkness, you are filled with the knowledge that anything is possible. In that instant, anything can happen. Anything at all. That's it. That's my favorite part. That exact moment waiting for the curtains to open, or someone to walk on stage. The anticipation creeping up like an active volcano ready to burst. I believe it is referred to as the overture. And that, my friends, is exactly how you should feel about your life.

You need to feel like anything is possible. You need to feel excited about what is about to happen. You need to live in the overture.

If you don't, you guys, then something's got to change. You have to find out what excites you and Do something about it. Life is going to pass us all in a blink. All of us. No matter how we live. So how do you want to feel day after day? Do you want to live for the big finish, or live in the excitement? Are you waiting for the pile of gold at the end of it all, or are you appreciating the silver linings along the way? You get to decide.

Chapter Four: Shift Your Thinking

Some New "S" Words

Here's what's helping me lately:

SHIFT- your mind and way of thinking. Literally shift it to see things differently, as a victor and not a victim. This does not mean to "change." That word is somewhat strong and permanent. Saying you need to change means saying there is something wrong with you. When you shift your thinking, it's a gentle way to look at your life from a different angle.

SIP- slow down and notice the little moments of happiness. Little things like the color of the sky, your kids' profile or laugh, a stranger saying hello. Stop looking for big, unrealistic, magical moments. Stop wanting for good things to jump out of nowhere and take away the struggle. Notice the beauty of your daughters' eyelashes, or the warmth from your morning coffee. You just need a little sip and a deep breath.

SIMMER- When you find those little moments, sit in them. Don't rush them away. Remain in that place as long as you can. Slowly inhale the simple, magical parts of your day and appreciate them. Linger there as long as you can and then put them in your pocket. I guarantee you will need to pull them out when things get murky.

SHIFT
SIP
SIMMER

Coffee, wine, sunshine, moments...do this with all the things that make you happy. Now, go do the things!

Growing and Shifting

I must have been dreaming about Buddhist monks because I woke up today with some deep thoughts. Maybe my head is finally catching up with my mindful morning practice because, boy do I have some questions. What if instead of trusting others, I learned to trust myself? What if by discovering who I'm meant to be and becoming more comfortable in my skin, it's not who they want me to be? Will they love me less? Will they still choose me? What if, while I grow and shift, they don't grow and shift with me? See what I mean? That's some heavy stuff to ponder.

These are raw and real questions that can keep me up at night. You know the kind that leave you questioning everything and bring along a heavy side of loneliness? I know. I'm going a little deeper today, but I actually think it's important and healthy to question your life. Not so much in a critical way. Definitely NOT in a way that causes you to look for flaws, that's not at all what I am getting at. I've never been a fan of Debbie Downer or Negative Nancy and I don't invite them out for cocktails. More so, in a vulnerable way that brings you and the people who love you to a better, more fulfilling and honest place.

The biggest surprise I've found lately, is that I am NOT the only one growing and shifting. I have somehow come to be friends with other men and women who are also feeling the shift. It could be our age, or maybe a few years of maturity and experience. But here's what I really think it is: I have CHOSEN to let these people in.

Writer Rikkie Gale's quote is SPOT on.

"I used to walk into a room full of people and wonder if they liked me. Now, I look around and wonder if I like them."

I've stopped worrying about trying to find adult friends. Collecting them or modeling their behavior so that I can "fit in." I no longer linger at school pick up or drop off hoping someone will invite me somewhere. I don't spend weekends wishing we had invitations for family gatherings with our kids. And guess, what? Our social calendar is more filled than ever. Sometimes, I turn down the invite because my family time with "just us," is the most valuable gift I know.

Jen Hatmaker did a podcast on "Fitting in" verses "Belonging." Holy moly, I have wasted too much time trying to be the funny girl and chime in with my random comments so that people would like me and I would fit in. (Obviously, I still have an absurd amount of random, sarcastic thoughts, no worries there, but I use them differently.) Now, I choose who I want to share my random thoughts with. At the end of the day, I have power over who is in my blanket fort. We all do.

I share my secrets, insecurities, and vulnerable feelings with the people who give me a sense of belonging. It is a mutual thing. If you are willing to be vulnerable with me, I am willing to be vulnerable with you. I've shared a lot in this book, but believe it or not, there are a lot of vulnerable thoughts I keep for myself, or the people I belong with. I am over "fitting it." I'm too old for it and just don't care to do it anymore.

It reminds me of middle school years looking for a seat at the "cool table," or any table really. When you are out of hope and full of shame, not sure where you fit in. Or, if you fit in anywhere. You know what's awesome about where I am right now? I don't even know where the "cool table" is. I don't know who is sitting there and it no longer matters. I found my own table at thirty-eight, half bald, with a body consumed by arthritis. And EVEN SO, even with all of that, I have created my own damn awe-inspiring table.

You should see the people at my table. They didn't necessarily look for me and I didn't go after them: we found each other. At a time when we needed something bigger, deeper, fuller, we saw each other shifting and thought "Hey, that's how I feel! So, it's okay to feel this way? It's normal to be shifting? Come sit here! Sit with me! Come to my table!"

Ahh. It's a really great table to be at. To feel heard, validated and then exchange the favor. Don't look for someone else's table, guys, make your own.

So, if you are going through a challenge in your life, find people you can be vulnerable with. Share it with them and then use it as an opportunity to surround yourself with those people. Because while all the people in your life won't be shifting with you, others will be. So, keep your eyes open. They are out there.

Side Note: Many people you love will NOT be shifting with you. No worries. Share with them anyway. This can be difficult as they may not understand your pain. But you have to understand it does NOT change their love. They WILL still choose you and maybe love you more for it.

Shifting Solo

Several times I have written about shifting. I really like this word because it describes what people do so well. Change is a much stronger word and so abrupt, as if it's that easy to change the way you've always thought about your life. You've heard the saying "people don't change," and for the most part, I believe that to be true. People can, however, shift. It's slight and easy to miss. Almost like looking to the side, seeing things from a different angle. I also feel like suggesting you need to change is suggesting that there is something WRONG with you and I don't like that. I strongly feel that we all need to shift our thinking, not change who we are. Because the people I know, the people I've met, are really good people. At the same time, we need to start looking at ourselves and each other from a different angle. Think of it like using a different focus or filter on your camera. It's the slightest movement, but it means everything.

Here's the hard part. Here's where things get messy and complicated and personal. Shifting your thinking is less complicated when life is happening to you. When you are the one at the root of a health/job/life issue. For example, me losing my hair. Yes, it affects everyone in life, but I am the one at the root of the hair loss (no pun intended.)

Naturally, going through a trauma, no matter how big or small, alters the way you look at yourself in the mirror. We've all heard the expression: pain changes people. For me, the way I see myself has shifted. Because I am at the root of it, I've had to dig deep for gratitude and self-acceptance. With the support of my family, friends, doctors, authors and God, I have come out for the better. But, what about the people in your life? What if they are not shifting with you? What if, while I am shifting in the left lane, they are still in the right? Can a marriage survive that? Will friendships slowly start to dissolve?

This is, by far, the most personal thing I have written about: my marriage. As I am shifting and becoming more confident in my physical and mental appearance, I fear my husband is not shifting with me. We are living this experience through two separate lenses. Not by any fault of our own, but because it is happening to me and he has to watch it with very little control. Not being able to "fix" it is very difficult for the people who love us.

Before any judgement begins, let me give you a little background on my husband. We met as two camp counselors in college and quickly found comfort in each other's company. He was that kid who always got in trouble and I was the teacher's pet. However different we may have seemed, we shared our values of faith, family, the importance of laughter and never taking life too seriously. We endured the long-distance college relationship and were eager to get married and start our life as a team at the innocent age of twenty-four. Since then we have taken life by the horns, constantly cheering each other to take risks, keeping family first. We have wrapped ourselves in laughter. A lot of laughter. He is ambitious adventure, and I am the calm home. He's seen me at my worst. Literally picked me up from the ground, squeezed the toothpaste when I couldn't and run out for coffee when we were out. He is a good man and I am proud to be married to him.

And still, there was a disconnect early on in my alopecia diagnosis. A solo shift on my end. I was shifting, and he was not shifting with me. And that scared the hell out of me. With both of us having divorced parents, we have always taken our marriage seriously. (I remember when we celebrated our seven-year anniversary and I told by parents that my first marriage lasted longer than theirs. Yeah, they did not share the humor of that fact.) So, where do you go from there? When you can feel the pull between you and your favorite person and aren't sure how to address it. It's like what started as a few drops of water between us was growing into a stream. How do you keep it from turning into a small river, or worse? How does a conversation begin when you're not even sure what's causing the pull?

So, I did what most girls do. I called a girlfriend. Because sometimes it's either that or burry it deep inside. We all know that does not lead to any solutions and likely creates bigger problems down the road. She calmed me down and reminded me that both my husband and I were knee deep in our own trauma. (He was currently going through the process to buy a company which was incredibly stressful and pain-staking slow.) It was consuming him, the way my hair loss was consuming me. We were not on the same page. But nobody was running out the door or closing the book. Like with many marriages much of our time together was with the kids leaving little time to have real conversations beyond sports schedules and spelling words. That's real life, though. No one to blame here. Raising half-decent kids is no joke.

This sweet friend that I've known since seventh grade and witnessed every stage of my life, not sure if that is lucky for her or not, is very rational. Her advice; slow down, give it a few days to simmer and if things don't smooth themselves out TALK to him. Tell him how you are feeling.

She's good at not making things bigger than they need to be. Plus, she knows my husband well enough to know that often, he just needs a day or two to blow off steam. With a gentle five-minute phone call, I felt heard, reassured and had a game plan.

The very next week, I had a girl's weekend away with friends who are as equally strong as they are vulnerable and believe in the power of sharing our stories. Somewhere between afternoon cocktails and the Chinese food delivery man, we moved on to the topic of marriage. Men, if this is new to you, please know we often talk about marriage. You can't be surprised by this. You may be surprised to know that although we all have complaints, women love their husbands and will gladly brag about them. The things we love about the men we married was a shared and valued part of our conversation, even if mine doesn't always put his coffee mug in the dishwasher. During this session, I brought up my concern about "Shifting Solo" and the women had all seen examples of this within their own marriage. It's part of being married a long time and essential to growing up. You are not meant to be the same person! We weren't the same people as we were when we got married at twenty-four. Life gets hard and we deal with struggles different at thirty-eight than at twenty-four and thank God for that.

After quickly validating both sides of our shift, they reminded me of some very important things:
- *He doesn't like to see me vulnerable, because he loves me and that's a hard thing to witness.*
- *He knows I hate pity or being "babied," therefore, he doesn't want to make me feel weak by coddling me.*
- *He might need me to tell him what I need from him because he's not a mind reader!*

Talk to him, duh. Just talk to him.

People don't have to shift together; they just have to be honest about their shifting. Apparently, you have to talk in your marriage! Ugh, I know. Such a simple concept and yet so hard to do. And I don't mean talk about where to go to dinner and when to head to Columbus next, I mean be vulnerable, real, raw conversation about actual feelings. Vulnerable conversations are some of the hardest, most uncomfortable conversations you will have. Guaranteed.

Marriage is hard. Being vulnerable is harder.

"Vulnerability sounds like truth and feels like courage,"
~Brené Brown.

But both are important to me and I plan on keeping each of them around. In order to do that well, I'll need to put my big girl pants on and have the hard conversations. There will be plenty more shifting in my life, if I'm lucky, and I'd like to do it with him by my side. We don't have to be in the same lane, as long as we are headed in the same direction.

My Invisible Cloak

Exciting news! I can become invisible.

I mean, I can be physically standing in the middle of the family room talking to my family and NO ONE even realizes I am in the room! Tell me I'm not the only one. It's beyond frustrating. The other day, I let them know I was heading to the grocery store and didn't get so much as a nod in response. Whatever. I got out of there looking forward to the freedom of strangers. And one hour later when I walked in the door, no one lifted their heads while they were happily coloring, or working on whatever task was important that day. As I asked for help unloading, they looked up in surprise. Oh, there you are mom. As if I was in the other room all along. Like, I magically appeared with a van full of groceries! I'm concerned they may think that little elves stock the shelves each night. Yet, my family seems to have no problem discovering all of the goodies in the pantry or fridge, like little gifts there to surprise them. Nope.

Hey. It's me, guys! Mom. Yeah, I'm the one that makes all those delicious, sprinkled with nutritious delights appear. Surprise! And I'm RIGHT HERE!

I know many of you can relate to the ridiculousness of the morning "let's get out the door before someone kills someone" routine. Right? This is another situation when I either magically lose my voice, or completely disappear from the kitchen. The number of times I calmly ask my children to brush their teeth and hair is like a chapter from every parenting book ever written. I mean, I could be mistaken for the Dali Lama with my mindful disposition. I've started my day with my own morning ritual in order to approach these stressful times successfully. (By successfully, I mean NOT dragging them upstairs by their toes and taking away their I-pads and TV rights until the end of time. Which I may or may not have done before.)

Deep breathe, ask them again. Did you finish eating? Did you grab a snack? Don't forget your lunch? Deeper breath. ask them again. Please put your shoes on and brush your hair. The boiling heat in my toes begins to build up in my ankles. I push it down and keep doing all the parenting tricks. But the problem is, I have turned invisible again. What the hell? How does this keep happening? I literally look around the room like an old school Candid Camera trick. I mean, there's NO way they can't hear me. And how, all of a sudden, did they being wrestling in the kitchen? And now, why is the dog jumping all over them as they are rolling on the floor?

How can I be so confused in my own house? Like, 4 seconds ago everyone was eating breakfast having a lovely conversation about what to do after school. I must be invisible. That's the only possible explanation! And now that I've asked them 497 times to brush their teeth and hair, I can feel myself physically shaking.

EXPLOSION. Then comes the screaming I promised I wouldn't do. The taking away of all of the toys they've ever owned. The Dali Lama would be so disappointed. But I tried, I tried so hard. Being invisible did it. I blame the magical cloak.

Then, and this is what really puts me in a whole other danger zone, they look at me like I'm the crazy one. Like I didn't ask them in a clam, after school special, Disney voice! As if I just walked in the room and started losing my damn mind for the fun of it. Then they have the audacity to speak to me? To look at me? With things like, "Okay. Geez, mom. You don't have to yell at us."

Yes. Yes, I did. Because to you I was invisible. And apparently the only way to break the invisible spell is to scream like a crazy person so that your children can see you again. It's unfair and insane. Sometimes I'm concerned that NO one sees me until I get to the gym. Once there, other adults say good morning or ask about my weekend. Thank God for these kind people. If not for them, I might walk around the whole day thinking I was wearing an invisible cloak. Like a freaking character from Harry Potter.

On the flip side, if something is wrong, if someone is sad, if a shoe is missing, I am the one who appears. I am the one who gets the first hugs and snuggles of the morning. I am the one my husband greets first each day. I am the one with all the answers. I am the holder of dreams, and the undeniable cheerleader. I am the keeper of secrets, the constant reminder that no matter what, you are loved. I am their home, their safe place, and their encourager. I wear that badge with honor, even if it is pinned to an invisible cloak.

This is yet another example of how I shift my thinking and hold on to gratitude. Because as much as my strange, invisible cloak can make my blood boil, I am everyone's #1. I am the go-to girl for the most important people in my life. I get all the good stuff even if I get a good chunk of the chaos as well. There's a good chance you are everyone that matter's #1, too. Wear that badge proudly because it will not last forever.

Defining Moments

I'm feeling a serious shift in my life. Not sure if it's my health or hair loss. There's also the issue of kids going back to school and living the final couple of years in my 30s. Cue in angelic choir. Probably a little bit of everything. Whatever it is- IT FEELS SO DAMN GOOD. Like a snake shedding its skin, I think I'm becoming who I'm meant to be. What?

Listen to this. Say it out loud to yourself.

"Rarely do you have the gift of knowing you're inside a moment that will be part of what defines you." - Brené Brown (Braving the Wilderness.)

For me, there were two moments:
Discovering the initial amount of hair in the shower drain.
And the day I literally let my kids dance in the rain.

One gut punching, crumble to the floor, struggling to breath moment. Ugh. You've had those. Nothing prepares you for that overwhelming grief. The world literally stops spinning and everything swirls around you. You don't know which way is up and you choke on the air around you.

The other is one good, tear jerking moment that makes you think miracles are possible and gum drops might actually fall from the sky. A moment in time that stops you in your tracks like God and Bob Marley holding hands and singing together "Everything's gonna be alright."

The combination of these few minutes of my life have led me to a deeply personal, peaceful place. There's still a lot I don't have control over. My hair is still falling out and my children are still ill-mannered little snack machines who might actually overdose on processed, crackery carbs.

But I'm at peace with all of it because it is EXACTLY what defines me. Can you think of a defining moment for yourself? Big or small. Heroic or tragic. This is what defines you. Forget "Mind Blowing." This is "Mind Shifting." I'm liking who I'm becoming and curious about where I'm headed.

Finding Gratitude in the Darkness

Things that bother me now:
- *Removing my hat for the National Anthem. (One of my favorite things is Tribe games. However, I've considered hiding in the bathroom for this and am relieved when we are late and miss it.)*
- *Going through security.*
- *Getting my height measured at the doctor.*
- *Desperately trying to clean out the shower drain after each shower, so my husband does not see what I left behind.*

You all can relate to the obvious insecurities people with hair loss go through. But these are the little things that throw a dagger in your day. Because I'm so damn tired of the little daggers in life, I'm choosing to shift the way I think about them

Why I'm grateful to Alopecia: (Did I use the word grateful?)
- *Somehow, I'm calmer in the intensity of life's storms. I take more deep breaths and let more things go. Even with my kids!*
- *I can finally take life one day at a time. Less planning, slower pace, even a little bit of "go with the flow".*
- *Honesty. I make less excuses to myself for my choices. In relationships and life- if it doesn't feel, sound or look like something I like- I will say so. It's also allowed me to connect with friends, new and old, on a deeper level.*
- *My kids are watching. They are learning from this and that is a wonderful thing. They are learning empathy firsthand by watching my struggle.*
- *Most importantly, it's made me grateful to the people in my life. Alopecia has pushed me to appreciate people and TELL them so.*

Once again, I'm not claiming to have "changed." Change is not easy or overnight for me. It's proof that I've shifted my mind and given myself the grace to see life a little differently. (Like the "upside down" in Stranger Things!)

Care a Lot About a Little

Recently, I was at a dinner party with some old friends. To be clear, they are "old friends" because we have been friends since middle and high school, not because we are actually old. Just to clarify. Anyway, one friend asked how I was doing. I love this friend so much because she is just the most real person you will ever meet. She doesn't sugarcoat life. In fact, she's the type of friend that couldn't lie to you if she tried. But her honesty is somehow always kind and gentle, so you are never offended. When she asks you how you are doing, you can literally feel the sincerity of her voice like the waves of the ocean. She's not asking to be polite; she's asking because she really wants to know. I'm not even sure she knows this about herself, but it's such a great quality and rare to witness these days.

So, you now understand that she's a gem and I always look forward to catching up with her, even if only once a year. I wanted to answer her with the same honesty she gives others. So instead of the usual, "Oh, everything's FINE!" (Insert eye roll and gag.) I thought of a deeper way to reply. Since I was already a glass of wine in, or maybe two but who's counting, neither of us could remember the exact verbiage.

I was talking with her about how losing your hair or going through any big transition changes you as a person. I'm a firm believer that pain changes people. I like the word "shift" better than change because I'm still not convinced people can completely change. I was explaining my shift and how I had to start looking at life differently. The best way I could sum it up was, "I stopped caring a little bit about a lot of things and started caring a lot about a few things." We both stopped a minute and thought about that. It made so much sense to each of us, yet in ways that applied to our very different lives. We even joked about how I needed to write it down so that I could use it in the future.

So, think about that for a minute. Much of my life, I was all over the place! Caring a little about this, a little about that. A little about all of the things. You know, juggling all the balls in the air! Unfocused and without clear priorities. Doing the daily grind like a headless chicken, without ever giving it too much thought. Anne Morrow Lindbergh, author of *Gift from the Sea*, describes it as our natural instinct to be givers. So many wheels spinning and us, at the center of it all.

"What a circus act women perform every day. It puts trapeze artists to shame. Look at us."

And it's true, isn't it? I'm not saying it as a complaint, more as a fact.

"Steady now!" Anne writes.

There are so many distractions. Never ending distractions. I'll have my mindful time carved out and, shit- I spill my coffee everywhere and then the kids wake up early. The moment I think I've got my day planned, the dog chews up a diaper in the hall trashcan. "How do we remain whole in the midst of the distractions of life?" Anne's asks. Obviously, there is no guaranteed answer, or we'd all be doing it. I have a hard time trusting anyone who claims they've got the key! I can't avoid the circus, hell, I love many parts of the circus. But I can shift my act in that circus.

Going through a life changing event, whatever it may be, really focuses you in on the important stuff. It sifts out the bullshit that just doesn't matter. There are just so many parts of life that simply don't hold value for me. Myself. My health. My family. A few friends. Boom. The end. I put all my energy into a few things. Less balls in the air. Smaller circus. No more putting my everything into everything! I was running my health into the ground and not completely living life the way I wanted. Shift into caring a lot about the few things that matter most.

I care a LOT about my morning routine. My quiet cup of coffee and time to think. Burning it out in the gym.

I care a LOT about my writing. My way of working through both the good and the bad. My happy place. The space where my head is clear, and heart is full.

I care a LOT about my children. Having hard conversations, playing more and building up their character. I could stare at their profile until my heart literally melts into a puddle at my feet.

I care a LOT about my marriage. Being honest, connected, vulnerable and putting in the time. Allowing myself to be supported and support him right back. Ride or die.
I care a LOT about carving out time for my friends and family. Letting them know they matter while we make memories, laughing and cheering each other through the journey.

That's it, folks. Sure, there are many more things that I care about. So many acts in the circus. But I've decided to put my time and energy into the few things I care about most. As I do this, most of the other things that are important really start to fall into place. Without the stress of needing to be everything to everyone, I am in a better position to care for myself and my people. Everything after that is a bonus.

I'll never pretend to have it all figured out. I don't have it all together and I never will. Thank goodness, right? I've decided that's not actually possible if you're doing it right. Because where I am in my life right now has taken a lot of work. I will have to continue to put in the work in order to keep my priorities straight. Goodness knows, as soon as the slightest hint of chaos starts seeping under the door, I can EASILY go back to my old ways of running around to put out fires. Toss all the balls in the air again, along with my sanity. I have to constantly to remind myself of my priorities, the few things I care about most. I'm like a little kid learning how to share toys. Slow down, take a breath, the world is not ending, one thing at a time, it will be okay. Breathe in what matters most, and breath out everything else.

Steady now.

Chapter Five: It's Not Just Your Grandma's Disease. Life with Rheumatoid Arthritis

Pain Is Pain

Beyoncé and Jay-Z. Goldie Hawn and Kurt Russell. Apple Bottom jeans and boots with the fur. Some things just go together, and we are all too interconnected to be thought of as solo at this point. Whether you deal with physical or mental pain: PAIN IS PAIN. Good days/Bad days - the struggle to get it all under control is the SAME!

Flash back to age thirty-three, I'm lying on the family room carpet, the beige California Berber pressed against my cheek. Total surrender to pain. My back, feeling as if metal rods were violently vibrating inside of it. My left foot squeezed by a vice. A constant cycle of squeezed and released pressure. (This is the relief I get with weekly injections and daily steroids?) I wanted to stay there, on that carpet forever. Crawl under the couch and hide away from the rest of the world, just me and my pain. No more six hour-days spent pleasing my middle school students and their parents. No more doing double duty as a mother of young children because of my husband's long hours at work. I had nothing to give. Take me out, coach.

You know in the movies when a bomb goes off and a victim lies there in shock, hearing nothing but seeing everything? As if time is standing still and you are at its mercy? I could feel the tears and sense my increased breathing as my husband picked me up off the floor. Through short, quick breaths, I know he carried me to bed telling me, "You can't do this anymore."

He had me. Not so much for the "for better" at this point. He was seeing me at my "for worse." It was one of the few times I allowed him to see me as I fell apart, completely vulnerable. My drained heart was filling up on pain and anger as I surrendered to all of it.

Running on empty was an understatement. I was tapped out and living a life of strike-outs. It was a wave your white flag, two hands in the air, kind of surrender. If my life were a game of poker, I would have folded and lost the farm. Something had to change. I was trying to please everyone, and because of that I was pleasing no one. Some say pain makes you feel more alive. Oh yeah, world, I just feel so freaking alive. BAM! Thanks for the reminder! Shout out to all of you fighting the good fight today. You are NOT alone.

No matter what kind of pain you are going through right now, or have in the past, pain is pain. It is a maddening deep hole without a light at the end of the tunnel. When you are in it, you are so far in it. Swallowed up like a snake's prey. You don't have to have Rheumatoid Arthritis to connect with me. Once you have met pain, you can understand it. But sharing and connecting with each other over pain allows that light to slowly seep back in.

Let Pain Make You Angry

Life is NOT all puppies and rainbows, folks. There are no unicorns hiding around the corner ready to hand you the winning lottery ticket. Most families fight their way through Christmas card photos sessions. We all sneak candy when no one is looking and then claim we ate a kale salad for lunch. Even the cutest puppy's poop on the floor, trust me. And, you can chase that rainbow until the end of time.

Honestly.

People can look all happy and cheery on the outside, but most are suffering some type of pain on the inside. Physical pain, mental pain, pain happens. It happens to everyone in many forms and shapes. (Every episode of Grey's Anatomy is a reminder of this. Am I right?) But for their own reasons, people aren't always open to sharing their pain. Yet, others share too much. Either way, we all know pain in some form or another.

If I am going to be brutally honest, which I am, living in constant pain can piss you off. It lights an angry fire that can make you want to lash out at others. Add a dose of steroids to that anger and…Watch the heck out, world! Been there and I'll be back there. You may know people who have chronic pain and notice that they seem angry or agitated. You bet they are! Science proves through different brain studies that living each day with nagging, stabbing or dull pain changes your brain. It literally makes daily responsibilities a struggle, leaving you helpless and dependent. That's where my anger creeps in.

It's true that pain has made me angry over the years. Not being able to open my kids water bottles or spaghetti jars is more frustrating that's you can imagine. Having to use my wheelie chair to get my students from recess feels both embarrassing and pathetic. Having to unclench my hands from shopping bags and crawl from the bed to the bathroom are daily events that piss me off. Here's the thing, though, BEING PISSED OFF MADE ME BRAVE. And it will do this for you, too. Take your pain and let it make you angry. Get angry. Take that anger and let it give you the fight you need to get back to living the life you want.

"Transformation happens in the pain," ~Glennon Doyle.

You will come out of it stronger and braver than you were before. I promise. It will drive you to do more, see more and live more. You just have to let the anger transform into fight.

Becoming the Hulk

How many of you have had to take Prednisone or some other steroid to help with one issue or another? It covers anything from arthritis, poison ivy, respiratory infections and even acne. The side effects of steroids can be brutal, right? From revenging hunger, water region, increased energy and my favorite, the jitters. I have taken some level of prednisone daily since 2010, with a small break during one of my pregnancies in 2011. After two years of tapering down, literally half a milligram at a time, I recently took my last pill in February of 2019. Although I have a relatively high tolerance to the side effects (lucky for me, I guess), steroids can TRANSFORM you.

In late August of 2013, I was diagnosed with rheumatoid nodules in my right lung. Throughout that summer, I had discovered strange and sensitive lumps on both of my shins. They were about the size of a quarter, raised like mosquito bites, yet had a purple, bruised coloring. You could assume, I was not to excited to rock shorts that summer. While at my general practitioner for treatment (after nodule on my right shin opened up) I informed the doctor that I was also having a stabbing pain in my right lung when I laid down. She was immediately uncomfortable with this and ordered a chest x-ray before I left. Being a mom of young kids, my toddler daughter got to witness the gushing nodules and lots of love from nurses when she could not be in the room. I have so much genuine appreciation for medical staff. They were on top of my situation all while keeping me calm and my daughter distracted and entertained. I received the results within an hour of leaving the x-ray. I specifically remember sitting on the couch with one of my sisters who was home with my son when I got the phone call. You know the kind of calls that literally stop you mid breath? When the doctor calls in her serious voice instead of the nurse practitioner or office staff? This was one of those.

She described that they had found growths on my right lung, one was considerably large and concerning. At this point there were three possibilities: the spread of my RA to my organs, an infection or Lymphoma. Obviously, none of these options were things I wanted to hear not to mention treat. I read all writing down the three diagnosis's and reminding myself to breath. She had already scheduled a CT scan for the next morning, which would confirm or rule out Lymphoma. I sat and told my sister the news knowing I would need childcare for my daughter in the morning since my little man had school and remember that the next day was also my daughter's birthday. The whole family would be coming over for dinner and all I could do was the next right thing.

After my sister left, I called my parents and husband while sitting on my bed, both kids napping, trying to get out the words in a slow, quivering voice. I saved the tears until the calls were made. Waited until then to fall into my covers and burry my head. Later that afternoon I made sure childcare was arranged and attempted to stay busy and distracted the rest of the day. Neither my husband or I slept much that night. At one point, before the sun was up, I rolled over to him researching the statistic of lung nodules and lymphoma and although they were very low, even the slightest risk was all consuming. I dropped off my son at school and my daughter at my dad's house and was in and out of the CT scan like it was as simple as going to the grocery store. I rewarded myself for my stress with an iced cappuccino and breakfast sandwich from Starbucks. I even ate some of the English muffin because if there was ever a day for gluten, this was it. I spent most of the day with a wondering mind, waiting for the call that would change my life in one way or another. Do you wish for a staph infection in your lung because it beats a Lymphoma diagnosis? Do you hope arthritis has taken over your organs because that's a better option? Talk about smiling your way through a family birthday dinner trying to focus on the kids or the food, but everyone's mind buzzing with the same thought. How sick am I?

The following day I did get the call that put my mind to ease, mostly. I did not have lymphoma which meant I was either dealing with some sort of infection or the spread of my arthritis. It means that my world would change, but it would not stop. So, I guess that's good news. I remember thinking that getting a dose of heavy antibiotics for an infection would actually be more a of a relief than knowing the RA was now in my organs. The next step was a lung biopsy so that the medical expertise could really get a better look at this. They would take a piece of my lung and check it to see if bacteria grew on it over time. If not, we were dealing with rheumatic nodules. If bacteria grew, then heavy antibiotics for the win!

After a few weeks, nothing was growing on the biopsy leaving the final diagnosis of be rheumatic nodules, or the spread of Rheumatoid Arthritis to my lung. The natural course of treatment is a high-dose, 4-month prednisone taper. In addition to this, I also inherited yet another specialist to my "medical team." You can imagine how fancy I felt to add a pulmonologist to my growing collection of medical experts. Yeah, I was THAT girl.

Immediately after meeting with an incredibly knowledgeable and experienced pulmonologist in Worthington, Ohio, we started off with forty mg per day for three weeks and with a plan to taper down as needed. Our goal was to use the high-dose prednisone to "zap" the nodules out of my body. Like some kind of superhero! This was the actual, medical term my well versed, expert doc used. He then referred to me as an "Auto-Immune Anomaly" after reading through my rap sheet of autoimmune diagnosis's. I graciously accepted my ultra-ego as compliment. (Please know that there are people fighting even bigger battles who are taking two and three times MORE than this per day for an unknown about of time. My forty mg and the battle I was facing was NOTHING compared to what others go through.) I felt relatively normal for the first few days likely because I have built up a high tolerance over the years, and the meds take three to four days to fully kick in and take over your body.

But on day four. Oh, friends. Day four, five and six. Holy vein-popping moly.

You should have seen me on the elliptical at the gym. You would have been like, "Damn. That girl is committed. She is serious about her fitness. I wish I had some of what she is drinking." I would have thanked you for the compliment and then kindly let you know that I was just juiced up on meds and then rambled on for twenty minutes about my medical issues and given you much more information than you have ever wanted or needed to know. You would have attempted to back up, ever so slowly and casually but I would not have gotten the hint. I would push on determined to tell you my story and burn off those jitters. Like a hamster on a wheel.

For another couple of weeks, I was able to burn off the "jitters" associated with prednisone at the gym or, by baking and crafting with the kids. I could mostly control the urge to move, scream or eat. And then, I wasn't.

I can still picture the afternoon in September playing with my kids after preschool pick-up. My son, who was four, was walking the well-worn line of acceptable behavior. I did my usual discipline routine and it resulted in him (and I) needing a "time out." I don't remember what he said or did next, as it is a bit of a slow-motion blur. Just another side effect of the drug that was healing my lungs! I picked him up and carried him to his room when he refused to go on his own. I wish I could claim that I don't understand his stubborn will power. But, alas, I do. It was at about that point when my clothes tore at the seams. The fabric shredded off my bulging muscles like cheese in a grater only to reveal the dark green skin I had been hiding. I was The Hulk, in a skinny, suburban housewife form.

Maybe a bit dramatic. Perhaps that's not totally accurate, but YOU GUYS, this is what it feels like when you are riding the prednisone roller coaster. You can feel OUTSIDE of your body. It's like you are watching it go down and have zero control about the unnecessary evil that's about to unfold. Just ask my husband. Actually, don't ask him. It's embarrassing enough for me to write about it.

The next picture that came into focus, there I was holding my son in the air. Raising him up like I was going to hang him on a hook. Or like when Mufasa holds up Simba for all the land to see. I remember thinking, "Oh. My. Gosh. What am the hell am I doing?" I can't imagine how that must have felt for him. I know it felt horrible and humiliating to me. I took a breath, calmly placed him on his bed and left the room. Immediately after walking out of his room I called my doctor and explained that I would not, could not carry on like this. I needed to start tapering down from this drug TODAY. I cannot do THIS anymore. And my doctor complied…mostly. He did give the go-ahead to lower my daily dose to thirty mg, but I would need to do that longer to ensure the nodules would be "zapped." He was a big fan of that term although just seconds ago I nearly "zapped" my son.

Prednisone can MESS with your mind and completely transform your personality. It can also lead to several long-term medical issues. However, many of us DEPEND on it to get through the day. Because it can also calm your skin, allow your body to move the way it was intended, and in some situations save your life. I am constantly trying to find the right cocktail of medications in order to lower my prednisone in-take, but it is a long and bumpy road. Be patient with people taking prednisone in order to deal with chronic pain because we don't like it any more than you do. Now, I'm off to burn away these "jitters" so I don't take them out on my people.

Don't Punch Strangers

So here we are. Again. My thumbs and pointer fingers are starting to curl, forming semi-permanent fists. Opening jars is no longer possible. Back to sleepless nights of tossing like a fish in attempt to ease the lower back aches and pains. Cringing as my knees, ankles and shoulders pop like kernels of corn.

It's the countdown month before a medical infusion. I don't need a calendar. My body knows and throws the pain at me as a cruel reminder. Friends and family may notice my fumbled texts with stubborn thumbs. But, for the most part, you will hear nothing from me.

Chronic pain brings anger, short temper (even more than my Irish ancestry gave me), and an overall pissed off step in my strut. Chronic pain is often described as an "Invisible Illness" for exactly that reason.

I look fine.
I act fine.
I must be fine.

My friends and I actually have a joke about this in regard to any life struggle. Aren't we all "fine?" I'm fine. You're fine. We are all so incredibly FINE! Here I am again, overwhelmed with the knowledge that I will live this way forever. The pain will come. It will go. But it will never be cured. It's a beast of a burden to walk around with Every. Damn. Day.

There are many good days. Many magical - full of love and life- kind of days. Days I pinch myself at my life and my people. And, damn! I've got the best people. Days when I look around and soak in gratitude everywhere. Many days when I feel strong and proud of my body.

But I'm not living in those days right now. Right now, I'm living in the pain and the anger of it all. Like that "I might punch a stranger in the face," kind of anger.

The next kind gentleman or sweet lady that gives me so much as a sideways glance or cuts me off in traffic is sure to get it in the kisser. You know? Tell me you know.

I've seen this pain before. Yet, I've also seen the beauty when it passes. I've been around enough to know, it does pass. The pain will fade. Everything is temporary. And I hold on to that knowledge until it does. Which is really is biggest most powerful thing. Just knowing. Being still. Repeating to myself "be still" over and over again.

Take a breath and wait for it to pass.

Woe Is Me Today

My usual mantra and even the name of my social media blog is "Woe is NOT me" and I take a lot of pride in that phrase. I don't believe in feeling sorry for yourself or playing the victim. Very few things annoy me more than playing the victim. But, not today my friends. Because, you know what? Woe IS me. And I'm kind of pissed off about it. (Please excuse my language, Dad.) Today, I am going to take five minutes and feel sorry for myself. That's okay to do sometimes, right? YES!

In that five minutes I'm going to be pissed that I can't...

- stomach my coffee on my new meds

- be patient with my husband

- keep up with my kids like I would like

- stomach coffee (yes, I know I said that already!)

- walk into a room and remember WHY I was there in the first place.

- keep track of my shopping cart at the grocery store

- keep up with my workouts at the gym

- stomach coffee on my new meds (Yes, this one is tragic.)

And in that five minutes I am going to wine, complain and cry an ugly, face-pulling cry. I remember when I would watch The Oprah Show in high school, and she would talk about the ugly cry. I was too young and inexperienced with the reality of laugh to know what she means by that. But twenty years later, the ugly kind of cry is my only kind of cry. So, for now, I will carry on about being annoyed at all the "Go for Your Dreams" posts all over Facebook. You go right ahead with your

"Positive Vibes Only." I, however, am going to sit right here and drown in my negative sorrows. Poor me.

I will continue to ignore all of the "but you don't look sick" comments. People. We all know everyone is fighting some sort of battle. Just because you can't see it does not mean it is not there. I will pathetically convince myself that I will be sick FOREVER and ever and ever. Nothing will change. Ever. My life is terrible. I hate everything. Blah, blah, blah. (A bit dramatic, I know. But, doesn't everyone feel this way at one point or another?)

Overwhelmed with frustration knowing that the combination of meds makes me sick while simultaneously allows me to physically move my body. Some sort of weird twisted medical mess, I guess. And when my five minutes is up, I am going to dry my eyes, put on a happy face, and go parent my ass off. I'm going to throw on my favorite sweat pants, take a beautiful California walk and cook up my favorite dinner, or perhaps take-out. The night has a high chance of ending with rocky road ice cream. When it comes time to literally pull yourself out that mood, you may need reinforcements. It's a matter of survival. You do you.

I've been here before, and one thing I know is "This too shall pass." DON'T PANIC! I don't need sympathy, prayers or hugs. Save those for the BIG stuff. Me? I just need five minutes! Five minutes to dump out all the bologna in my brain with tears and erratic screams. A little time-out is all. Tomorrow is for positivity, but today I get five minutes of pity.

Infusion Day = My Draft Day

Prepping for my next medical infusion tomorrow is like an athlete prepping for draft day. It's the day you put all your hopes and dreams into that one moment. Just hoping that it's everything you want it to be. Will it live up to the hype? Will it be a let-down? Do you stay positive or prepare yourself for the fact that it may not work out after-all? And then you start all over...again...

Like an athlete, I am very aware of what goes into my body. I focus on combining REAL and HEALTHY foods with other natural supplements. I follow an anti-inflammatory diet and exercise, nothing high impact though (because that would counteract everything, I'm doing to help my joints, plus my dad would be mad and I hate upsetting him!) Mostly I concentrate on Piyo, Pilates, muscle conditioning and interval training- sometimes solo, sometimes with my senior friends. Luckily, I am out of the gym before the Silver Sneakers classes get started. Not that I won't be a part of that crew one day. Just not today. When that time comes though, you better believe I will be in the front row and ROCK that class. White orthopedic shoes and all!

Although there are days when none of those things are an option due to the damn RA. Blah. Blah. Not going there today. No five minutes of pity needed this round. Somedays I deadlift weights, other days I can't tie my shoes.

Balance.

Unlike Draft Day, an infusion is six hours in a chair hooked up to an IV of miracles. You are in a room filled with these chairs and fellow "players". (Once again, I bring down the age average a good twenty years.) It's different for everyone, but for me taking Rituxan I do one dose tomorrow and then another six-hour infusion two weeks later. Usually that will last you anywhere from six months to a year. For the record, there are many different types of medications for autoimmune diseases all which require different infusion schedules. (I know this because I've taken a few.)

As my doc told me last week with a hug and kiss on the cheek, I am a rare case, so I am getting my dose after only four months. It is supposed to provide relief longer than four months and it's a good possibility that I may be developing anti-bodies making the medication less effective. SWEET! Record-breaker! Rule defier! Lucky. Lucky me. My glass is half full, right? It's actually overflowing my cups it's so full, but I have to consciously remind myself of that. It's a shame this "luck" doesn't come in handy with the lottery or even getting tickets to the Ellen show!

So, for now I am going to chug my water today because the infusion does leave you feeling pretty wiped out and "fuzzy." I am going to look forward to the 120 mg of prednisone they fill you with before the meds. (One armed push-ups here I come!) And I will be able to rest thanks to my mother-in-law being in town to help with the kids and dinner. I really am pretty lucky after-all. Mostly, I am going to hope this med "drafts" me to six months or more of health. Bring it.

Just One of Those Days

One of those days where you feel like you're going to be sick FOREVER. (Foreva eva? Foreva eva? I love Outcast.) This leaves you with an overwhelming feeling of hopelessness. Forever is a freaking LONG time to feel like CRAP and it becomes very hard to see life any other way. The future is a cloudy haze with little signs of clearing. So, what do you DO? What the heck do you do?

Reach out.

Reach out to friends, family, the lady at the checkout counter. Whatever. Just, reach out and touch someone. Metaphorically speaking of course. I would suggest more of a conversational connection rather than a physical one. The idea is to let them know you are struggling. Don't hint at it- tell them with actual words.

Listen. Listen to these people. Listen and look at their words and how they describe you. Let them compliment you and remind you of your strength. Words can CLEAR the clouds. Words are the most powerful thing I've found as an empowering force and a reminder of gratitude.

In the last week, I've been gathering documents for teacher certification in CA (that's another story.) Some of those include letters of recommendation. I asked some former co-workers and current friends I tremendously respect and who are at the top of their game, to write me letters as required by the state of California. Please know that the people I asked know me. They know me very well both personally and professionally. The good. The bad. The highs and the lows.

Do you ever feel like the universe has your back? Like, just when you need a little pick-me-up, or reminder of what matters most: bam! That gentle nudge or hug honest to goodness shows up in your mailbox. It was a goosebumps moment for because I received them all within the last few days. I read and reread them three or four times needing so desperately to take them in. Their letters reminded me who I REALLY am. The type of person who goes above and beyond and loves without regret. A person who is NOT sick, NOT bitter and not a victim.

I needed reminding today. I needed to reach out, and then look and listen to their words. We all need reminding sometimes and we need to remind others what we love about them. My future is a little less cloudy today. (Despite another catastrophic rain storm headed to CA.)

Superhero Status

It's a bird, it's a plane...no it's me. Apparently, I'm a superhero.

Did you know that my cough and abdominal muscles are so powerful they actually cracked my rib? These abs flex with enough steam to push through human BONE. I know! I guess all those Pilates and PiYo classes really paid off.

Life throws fireballs and gives you mixed bundles of reality. It's funny and depressing at the same time. This is the second time I've cracked a rib due to weak bones. The first time it was a simple sneeze. A sneeze that felt like a gunshot! The pain was so intense I actually looked around my car to see if I had been shot, no joke. Years of prednisone and other heavy meds can do that. They can mess up your winds and get you off course. But I've got too much good stuff going on here to let the change of winds mess up my route.

So, I simply adjust my sails. Slow down. Breathe a little slower. Sail on!

And just like that, I received a kitchen towel from my loving mother-in-law for Mother's Day. Stitched into the aqua blue fabric are the words "When you can't control the wind, adjust the sails." `Talk about perfect timing! Apparently, she "saw this and immediately thought of me." Little did she know that looking at it hang in my kitchen today was exactly what I needed.

Clinical Remission

Overwhelmed. Overemotional. Overjoyed. ANNNDD... "Living in Clinical Remission."

I know there are a lot of skeptics out there. People who might roll their eyes when I post "clean recipes" or lose focus when I talk about living gluten and diary free, downing ACV, fish oil, or handfuls of vitamins.

I know. I know...it can be annoying. And it might not be your thing. But then my rheumatologist looks over my blood work, drops her jaw, turns to me and calmly says "your blood work shows clinical remission levels."

The universe pauses for a moment. You ask her to repeat it. And she does.

What does that mean? Being on intensive meds requires blood work every eight to twelve weeks for various levels of toxins. WITH medication, usually there are still signs of inflammation and other issues in the blood and it is very difficult to level them out. For the FIRST time, ALL of my tests (almost twenty) show everything in the low to mild range of normal. It is the best my blood work has looked in years and it is no luck of fate. It is not simply "by chance."

Yes, this is WITH medication. We don't know what my levels would be without medication and won't for some time. So now we slowly lower SOME of my meds. Little by little. With close moderation, of course.

Don't be a skeptic, you guys.

I've spent the last few months focusing on what goes into my body both physically and mentally. Positive thoughts, persistent diet and exercise and the perspective that things could always be worse. Those of you who have kept up with me the last few years know that I have annoyingly dedicated my focus to a humorous, healthy lifestyle. And the proof is in the pudding (or blood work, I guess.)

Make a choice. Live your best life. Or, don't. I'm not giving up.

I'm Fine. Totally Fine

Chronic Pain People- enough with being Superheroes already!

When you live a life with daily, chronic pain, no matter how severe or intense, you get used to "sucking it up." You over use the term "I'm fiiiiiiinnne" and carry on with your day. Trust me. I get it. There are few things more annoying than a winy, poor me, I'm a victim type of personality. Nobody likes a Debbie Downer. So, yeah, I'm fine! Totally fine! Right...

Until you're not. My family and I have just completed the two-and-a-half-week road trip from California to Ohio. We were all loaded up in a minivan with our 14-year-old chocolate lab and a suitcase of germs. Overall, it was an absolute trip of a lifetime stopping in amazing cities and taking in all of the sites together. Now, here I am in my hometown, surrounded by my people, and struggling through my latest diagnosis...damn pneumonia. (I call it "damn pneumonia" because I've dealt with a lot of illnesses in my thirty-seven years, and THIS one is a beast. Plus, I feel like my Grandmom would say it which is comforting.)

I should have known when I couldn't keep up with my kids while we hiked through Estes Park in Colorado. I should have known when the fever and chills set in when we snuggled into our cabin at the YMCA family summer camp. (Which I highly recommend, by the way.) I could have flashed back to when my daughter was down with a fever in Monterey and I didn't leave her side with my compromised immune system. Finally, when I developed a cough that started in my baby toes moving up my tense body ending in flashes of light behind my eyes. Some of the most intense pain I've experienced yet. (Like, curl into the fetal position on the floor kind of pain.)

I should have listened to my body. I should have slept and not offered to drive for hours at a time clenching the steering wheel in pain. All the while insisting I was fine. But, I didn't. Because so many of us keep the mentality of "suck it up buttercup." We just want to keep pushing through. I didn't want to miss a moment or the magic of the trip. And now here I am, literally at times gasping for breath like I'm breathing through a pin.

Listen to your body and drop the Superhero act. Don't be like Angie. Be human and be smart. Monday is a great day to go back to being a badass. (Or, maybe Tuesday depending how quick the medication kicks in.) There is no rule about being tough and goodness knows that there is no prize. Your people will take you in and actually find value in getting to take care of you. Every now and then, let them be tough for you. It seems to keep coming back to letting that shit go. The idea of being a CONSTANT Superhero...let it go, my dears. Just let it go.

Peace Out, Prednisone!

I'm showing you the door. Or, at least I'm trying to.

So, I'm up in my daily number of pills, but down in dosage. AND the majority of my pills are healthy supplements. Win! People with chronic illness constantly juggle various meds, diet changes, workout regimens and supplements. What works one month, may not be effective the next. Much like the eating habits of by six-year-old.

I have accepted the fact that I will live my BEST life with the marriage of both eastern and western medications. But prednisone is like that ANNOYING roommate that just won't leave. They pay rent, keep beer in the fridge and make the occasional funny joke. But when it comes down to it, they are obnoxious and lazy. They have overstayed their welcome, yet we depend on them to make life work.

I have not gone ONE day without prednisone for almost 8 years. I've flirted with five to sixty mg and like Lady Gaga sings, "you and me could write a bad romance." My long-term relationship with prednisone has led to fatigue, weak bones, digestion struggles, hair loss, etc. Luckily, I have not yet developed a "man voice." So, all things considered...

Don't forget the weak autoimmune issues which has given me the opportunity to battle problems even your grandmother hasn't seen like broken ribs, shingles, pneumonia, and leg and lung nodules. Yes, supplements can balance some of these symptoms, and you all know I live a healthy lifestyle! But my goal (for the last three years) has been to get prednisone the hell out of my house!

At the point of writing this, my daily routine included Rituxan infusions, Arava and a double fist of supplements and ACV, my doc granted me permission to start the eviction process!

I'm currently on week four of 4 mg/day of prednisone, which is HUGE. The first 3 weeks my body was like, whoa. What's happening here? Tingling feet, hands and fingers curling up, bringing Ibuprofen back into the mix to numb the lower back pain, and a serious case of the grumps.

But this is a new week and my body is slowly starting to adjust. Our bodies don't like and will fight change - in any situation. Next week, I'll go down to three and, fingers crossed, my body will accept it

Day by day. It's not easy to evict a roommate of over seven years. But, it's BEYOND time. Buh-Bye. Don't let the door hit you on the way out, roomie.

Freak Out, Forgive and Try Again

I just woke up like this.

Ever just wake up pissed off, not for any particular reason? Just pissed. (Even at thirty-eight I can still hear my parents asking me not to use that word. My apologies, but I just can't come up with a better description.)

It could be the weather, but the sun has been out and the sky is blue. It could be the stresses of normal life, but I realize I'm lucky to have the stresses that my life brings. It could be that my hands are cramping up, and my fingers are the shape of sausage links looking more and more like an ad for RA. (Hey, maybe that's a career move!) Maybe it's the numbing, tingling in my toes at night making sleep a struggle. It is likely, the stiff hips and knees attempting to slow me down and keep me from "showing up" to my life.

So, in attempt to be a responsible adult, I head to the gym to blow off some steam and flush away my Debbie Downer attitude. But there it is again. The heavy, damn struggle that is chronic pain. Keeping me from going full steam ahead, prodding me with little reminders that RA is such a pain in the ass. (No pun intended.)

I hate making excuses. I believe in mind-over-matter and that EVERY single body can do a hell of a lot more than you think. But I also believe that pushing through certain pain leads to long term damage. I know when to be patient with my body and take it down a notch, but man does it piss me off. And it definitely does not mean that I always listen to its request to slow down. I pride myself in being tough. I know I'm not intimidating to look at. I also know I pushed through forty-five minutes of burpees this morning and then headed to Spin.

For me, admitting that I physically can NOT do something, is admitting defeat and I have never been a good loser. Don't tell me I can't do something. I had to pause several times yesterday, to 'Be Still,' take a breath and push back the tears.

Not because the pain was too intense. But because I knew that specific pain, and I understood it was telling me to stop. To quit. Aw, hell not. I wasn't having it.

So, what do you do when you are faced with that wall? Where one side of the wall is what your body needs, and the other is what your body wants? I wanted to go home, drink coffee, eat a cake, listen to some Mumford and Sons and throw a kick-ass pity party. Who doesn't love a good old-fashioned pity party? Instead, I toned it down, wrapped up my first class and headed to Boot Camp determined to finish out my routine. I cursed my way through box jumps as I heard my Rice Krispie knees screaming at me. That was a bad call. I know. Some people call me stubborn. Can you believe that? Box jumps are really not a good idea when I am having a flare in my knees. Don't lecture me, though, I was ANGRY.

What's done is done.

I will remind myself to be kind to my body. Be patient knowing that my next infusion is 2 weeks from tomorrow. Until then, I will begrudgingly increase my prednisone and stick to lower impact options.

I will focus on all the GOOD going on around me. My little man is turning 8 this weekend. My dog turned forteen and is still walking. The sun is out, and my husband brought home a good bottle of wine the other day that I just might break into. Not, like, right now. Since it's before noon.

Freak out, forgive, and try again tomorrow.

Privacy Curtain Dreams

The first full day of spring 2018 is here and I'm incredibly busy living my best life.

You guys, the Cleveland Clinic infusion room is so fancy! Its crisp, clean whites are mixed in with warm neutrals. Everyone coming in for treatment has their own snuggly little section with a recliner, two tables and an extra chair inviting enough to make you forget about the IV poles, needles and other medical equipment. Each soft, beige recliner comes with an attached tv screen, as many pillows and blankets as you request and ear buds (although I brought my own from home.) The kind-hearted, honest-to-goodness, happy to be there nurses offer you snacks and make small talk. I turn down the snacks since none are gluten free but accept some water. I'm happy to pass on the snacks because I came fully prepared with my own. It's not my first rodeo!

I've been in three different hospitals for infusions and this one, by far, surpasses the others. I've had comfortable set-ups before as well as awkward rooms without TV or conversation. When living out west, I had nurses that needed two or three pokes to get the IV in correctly with little apology. But not today, not in Cleveland! I watched as the other nurses and patients in the room caught up like old friends meeting up for happy hour cocktails and thought, I want to be a part of that. And now I am! If there was a contest for infusion room coziness and happy faces, Cleveland Clinic Main Campus would hold that title all day long.

Here are a few of my favorite things about infusion day:
Coffee
A good book
Pad with "I Tonya" ready to go
My own tv to watch a bit of the Today show.

Plus, I didn't realize the luxury of a recliner! (Does that realization reflect my age?)

The biggest victory of all? Cue angels and birds singing "Hallelujah". The privacy curtain.

Um, why do I not have a privacy curtain in my own home? This is something we, as humans, should invest in. Can you imagine sitting in a recliner at home, kids start arguing, and you pull your privacy curtain closed? Sorry kids. I can't see you. Figure it out. I'm behind my privacy curtain watching my shows. Honestly, I found them on Amazon, but it's a little tricky to figure out how to hand them in a standard living room or office space. Please contact me if any of you engineering minded people can mastermind, or MacGyver some type of privacy curtain for the home.

Until then, I've got snacks, blankets and peace here. This place makes me feel like queen of the autoimmune world and ready to kick its ass. Also, I've decided against cooking dinner tonight. I think we can all agree that take-out is an important part of my recovery. It goes without saying that French fries are essential.

Granted, when I leave here I'll be wiped for a day or two. By Friday, or maybe Saturday, Sunday at the latest, I'll be ready to take some numbers. But, first, movie and a nap.

Surprise! No One is Coming to Rescue You

No one is coming to save you, guys. Whether you are struggling mentally or physically, pain is pain is pain. But you CAN make the choice to save yourself. You can choose to put in the work, mentally and physically. I'm not going to lie, it's a lot of work. Possibly more work or at least harder, more different from work you have done before. And it is dark and heavy. But, it's your choice to make every single day. Yours alone.

It's so easy to lose your mojo. Isn't it? Some days you wake up ready to take on the world and get to it. Other days, nope.

I lost my mojo today. I woke up agitated. I was tough on my kids, gave my husband grief when it was not needed. I was less than pleasant and even further from precious than usual. But I willed myself to the gym on pure stubbornness. Sometimes, being stubborn can be your best quality, with my shirt inside out. Thank you, Monday.

I have learned a few things in this process of getting to know myself. I know now that I have to read, listen to and do things that inspire me and remind me of my mojo. It's just so easy to forget. Today I needed reminding like a smack in the face. I needed to be shaken and snapped out of that dark place. Get it together, girl, get it together.

Some days it's a Podcast, song, walk, sweat fest at the gym, or a good book. Other days, it's a Hallmark movie, ice cream and sweat pants. Whatever. Yes, I find my mojo in Hallmark movies. They make me feel warm and cozy and all of the happy things. Who cares if I can predict the plot within the first 38 seconds!

Today, it was a little "Greatest Showman" music to wrap up the last hill in spin class and a reminder from a supportive friend. She reminded me of what my goals are and where I want to go. Like a robot with an "on" button, I turned it around. She was right there when I needed someone and said the thing I needed to hear. I was ready for her, too. So often there are people in your life who are there.

Physically and emotionally there and telling you the things you need to remember about yourself, but if you're not listening then you will miss these opportunities. You have to look for these signs and absolutely be open to accepting them. Don't accept them with a sarcastic comment or by shrugging them off, which we so often do. If you're uncomfortable with the compliments, a simple "thank you" will do the trick. But you should not push these truths away. Instead, say "thank you" and hold on to it.

Now I'm home after a good work out, listening to Podcasts that motivate me and putting in the work. I didn't want to do it. I didn't really like it. But I showed up anyway and that's where magic hides. Those moments when you push through even though it's SO much easier to give up. Simply showing up for the hard stuff: parenting, working, pain, relationships.

"Be messy and complicated and afraid and show up anyways." ~ Glennon Doyle.

Be your own hero with your own kind of mojo because we've all got it in us. You can overcome so much more than you think. You can own your struggles from crappy Monday mornings to more serious chronic health issues.

Find what inspires you and drink it in! Show up and put in the work.

(Now, I'm off to buy some pumpkins to carve with the kids tonight because THIS family did not make it to the pumpkin patch. I know. I know. No magical memories to post on social media this year. But next year we will kill it with our fall magical memories. There will be cute plaid, puffy vests or something adorable and precious.)

You Have to be a Warrior to Love Someone with a Chronic Illness: A Thank You Note to Those Who Love Us

Everyday. All the time. I am reminded that I am a fighter. A Warrior. A force to be reckoned with in the face of pain. Many of us are fortunate enough to feel the constant support and encouragement from people in our home and beyond. We know we are lucky.

This intense support has allowed me to understand the power of being GRATEFUL. The reason we are so grateful, at least for me, is due to my abundance of unsung heroes.

Every time I fight, they fight.
When I pray, they pray.
When I feel frustrated, I know they feel it too.

They watch me suffer and fight, all the while feeling helpless. Thank you for being my Warriors. I am grateful that you do NOT pity me. There is NO coddling between warriors. Thank you for supporting all of our innovative, boarder-line crazy, holistic experiments and putting up with changes in our diets and strange chickpea brownies you try to choke down while laughing. I appreciate the way you smile and nod when you come home to zoodles instead of noodles for dinner. How you know to fill up on gluten and refined sugar outside of the home.

Thank you, warriors, for reading or at least pretending to read, the countless articles I send out hoping to find a hidden explanation or cure for chronic pain. The random texts and memes of people with arthritis. And when I look at you with a twinkle in my eye because an essential oils representative is coming to share some ideas, you schedule your lunch break around the meeting so that you can attend. That's a Warrior!

While I am fighting to stay positive and look for hope, you are fighting equally hard to stay hopeful for me. Thank you for being patient when I need you to be patient. For walking away when you know the meds are talking and for letting me break down when I need my five minutes. (Or ten, forty-five, whatever.)

You see, the gift of the warrior is not only the "fight" they bring to the game, but also the ability to catch you when you fall. And goodness knows, we all fall. I am surrounded by warriors, and I am GRATEFUL for it.

Thank you to those of you who read this. You are, no doubt, warriors for someone in your life. I guarantee, even if they don't or can't say it, YOU MAKE A DIFFERENCE.

We are ALL Warriors. Thank you!

Chapter Six: Beautiful, Messy Parenthood

To the Pickers

To those who pick up the pieces, I see you, I hear you and I feel you.
Whether solo, or with a partner, widowed or somewhere in-between. Whether supported or stranded.

I see you there, picking up the pieces. And there are so many unspoken pieces. Making sure the kids are clothed, meals are fed, sports are played, and little ones are transported to all of their places.

I hear you, taking your deep breaths. Settling another argument or playing another game of make-believe all while building up confidence and wiping away tears.

I feel you, slowly sipping your coffee. Working so desperately hard to be the never-ending support of your spouse and children. Taking one quiet moment for yourself before madness ensues.

You may or may not have the perfect back to school sign for first-day-of-school pictures. Your kids may or may not have an environmentally friendly lunch box organized with all the organic, non-GMO ingredients. You may want to yell and scream about how everything is a mess right now and you don't know where to turn.

Yet, there you are.
With a smile.
Picking up the pieces.

You may feel you are fighting a lone battle, but you are an army of many. We juggle. We dance. We support. We glue. Rarely discussed- it's our job, as pickers.

I know your struggle, the frustration, occasional anger and the fear that the pieces are too heavy to hold. Too slippery to keep afloat. Too lonely to carry on.

One piece you've NEVER dropped. Never needed to pick up, is love. That is one you carry every day. That's the one that matters. (Most of those other pieces were meant for Pinterest anyway.)

As you sip your coffee, or tea (organic or not), or protein drink- PICK UP YOUR PIECES FIRST. Your pieces are the most important of all.

The world will not end, the children will be okay if you let a few pieces fall now and then. Just, don't let them be yours.

Stickers and Demerits: A Day in the in Life

of Elementary Music

In my experience, there are days when one child gets dismissed with a personal teacher escort. But, the other? The other child runs out as if she spent the day petting puppies and riding unicorns over the rainbows.

Call it ironic. Call it balance. I call it B.S.

Apparently, my older child was enjoying the sound of his voice a little too much in music class. He had a lot to share or at least a lot to say to his classmates today whether or not they wanted to hear it. Even the teacher, at this point, had grown tired of his need to chime in and be heard. So much so that the standard three to five friendly reminders for quiet voices, were NOT effective.

Because my son is above school rules, right? He gets a free pass for that charming smile of his? Nope. Huh Uh. No way. I will take the teachers' side EVERY SINGLE TIME. I know how the stories transform by the time the student gets home into some sort of mystical mystery of "I don't know why!", "I was just sitting quietly" or "It wasn't me!". Most of us have been there. Because we have been there, we are less likely to believe total innocence.

Yeah. Sure, buddy. (Another curse of a teacher kid.)

Luckily, my little riot rebel already knew the truth was out. He had the school's response in ink laying on the kitchen island. There was no denying it now. Punishment received. The first second grader to get a demerit this school year. Granted, he did make it to October. High-five for fabulous parenting! Once home, we talked about the day's drama and how HE could do things differently the next time he was enamored with the sound of his own voice. We brainstormed other ways he could move or stay busy if he was feeling the urge.

However, instead of insightful feedback, he had two bits of second grade wisdom:

1. "I can't control it mom! Except at sports. I can control talking there so you don't need to take that away."(He has lost sports before and did NOT like it- which makes me like this punishment even more.)
2. "Mom! I was really funny though. I had my friends cracking up!"

Oh. Okay. Well in that case, buddy-CARRY ON! As a sarcastic family, this was the response in my head. However, I knew enough to keep it there. In the midst of this semi-serious conversation, the little lady of the house walks in bouncing around, giggling like a 6-year-old does.

"MOOOMMMM! I earned a sticker today!"

Pause. This is a vital parenting moment. How do you address the child who needs encouragement while disciplining the other? This is one of those situations where you need to tread lightly and choose your words wisely. Knowing I needed to give her some of my parental attention, I responded with "Oh, how exciting" and asked how she earned a sticker.

"It was in music class, mom! Because I was the BEST listener in the class!" she exclaimed.

Wha? Wait? Huh?

Sometimes, God, the universe or possibly both has the best sense of humor with the most precise timing. My son and I both threw our hands in the air. Ultimate surrender. My son turning his grimace into an open mouth, full teeth smile and yelling, "Are YOU kidding me Lucy?"

And we all fell on the floor in laughter. Rolling around the ground making eye contact and immediately losing ourselves in the moment again. This is how we do life. A tangled web of emotions and irony. Two kids. Same parents. Same music teacher. Same stinking day. Yet, two TOTALLY different outcomes.

Stickers and demerits.

We fail. We win. We hug and laugh. But mostly, we try again tomorrow.

So, You Don't "Fit in the Box?"

A letter to my son who doesn't "Fit in the Box".

From day one, you were the kid who was on "red" in those annoying preschool behavior charts. As if every child's success could be wrapped up into a damn color wheel. You and I both hated those color charts. The ones that determined if you were a "good" or "bad" kid. By three years old, you labeled yourself a "bad" kid simply because society did and did so very loudly with little wiggle room. Granted, you were a pistol. Stubborn. Intense. And if not given stimulation, you would find it. You were not, nor have ever been a child who sits quietly and goes with the flow.

So, we made a rule. The first thing I would say at pick-up was,
"No matter what, I still love you."

Before I asked about your day. Before the teacher could fill me in on any issues. I stopped you. Hugged you and asked you to repeat our rule. You would say "No matter what, you still love me". This has carried on over the years as a rule needed for all of us. Because in this family, no one is perfect.

I wish society didn't want to put you in a "box", sitting quietly with your hands folded in your lap. I wish society celebrated your undying intensity to take on any challenge that comes your way. It would be nice if people saw your brilliant ability to catch and throw sarcasm with the best of them. I wish society didn't treat your need to be physically active as a negative but accepted it as part of childhood. All the labels. All the stereotypes. It's too much for you and it's too much for me.

If I could, I would give you a world where you show love with physical connection without being seen as "aggressive." Here, people would not see your fearless nature as reckless behavior. I would give you a world where being headstrong and confident wasn't treated as an act of disrespect. In this world, kids sitting with I-Pads wouldn't be considered as obedient, while you're sitting at the next table noisily telling me about your day and dealing out cards for another game of Michigan Rummy. People would smile at you, not roll their eyes as you exploded in a celebratory victory cry. I would surround you with people whose voices filled you with support and acceptance. You would feel that you are enough just as you are.

As you grow, may you continue to find your people. Because they are out there. These people will take you in, feed off of your energy, be challenged by your intensity and laugh with your humorous spirit. They will be better because they knew you. I know I am. May you find safety and comfort in these bonds because, you will need them in life. Your people. They will love you with the same intensity you love them. So, give them your whole heart. Don't be afraid to let down your guard and let them feel your soft, gentle-giant of a heart.

No one should be in a "box." And I wouldn't want you any other way. Life WILL be hard. But I will love you harder. You WILL make mistakes. But you will learn from each of them. Not everyone will understand you. But the ones who matter most will see the intense insight you bring to the world.

And no matter what, I still love you.

Birthday Lesson - "Be Still"

I love turning thirty-seven and I'm not afraid to admit it. Yeah, I'd prefer less wrinkles and grey hair, but whatever. I'm letting that go. (Well – not totally. I will continue to use quality facial products and color my hair until the end of time! I don't need to let it ALL go.) I didn't love thirty-three, thirty-four or thirty-five because I was reaching my mid-30s and naive enough to think that it was all downhill from there. Time to invest in Botox and push-up bras. "I'm SOOO old. Where did the time go?" Blah. Blah. Blah. Oh, young girl, if you only knew.

The past year has been a year of struggle in EVERY way. I've struggled with my health, personal relationships, motherhood and overall happiness. I've had my loneliest and most painful moments. I'm not looking for sympathy or encouragement here – puh-lease. Quite the opposite.

The struggle of year thirty-six allowed me to discover the beauty to simply "Be Still." Breathe in. Listen to your body, heart, and perhaps your God. Then breathe it all out. Let that stuff go. Just. Be. Still. There are subtle, yet powerful messages in the stillness if you listen. Those calm moments have become my safe place. And now I am stronger and happier than before.

Here's the kicker: PEOPLE notice. Not just any people, MY people. More specifically, my little people. I came downstairs this morning to find a birthday card my son had made on his own. After quickly trying to decipher his spelling, which is no easy task when your kids are standing in front of you with hopeful eyes. You've got to be sure you get it right. He had written, "*I love you a lot and a happy birthday to you. My mom is strong and powerful. My mom is a superhero and pretty.*"

Keep in mind this is coming from a six-year-old, guarded little person. My boy. We struggle to connect and relate to each other many times. I often feel like he takes me for granted with little regard for how much I put into our family. But kids speak the truth. And his truth proves that they are watching us. Our every move and hearing our every word. We might think we are hiding our feelings and our pain, but these little people see it and feel it too. However, this is NOT a bad thing! LET THEM.

I am glad he knows that I've had some "lows" because he witnessed me push through it. My little man watched me fight for the ability to CHOOSE happiness. He called me a freaking Superhero! He called his mother "strong and powerful." When most days he tells me "you don't make sense", or simply responds with the word's "poop" or "fart." While he might share the little stuff, he's hearing the big stuff. The good stuff that will actually mold him as a person and how he sees the world. My God. Could there be a better gift?

He knows that you can have a hard time physically, or mentally and still RISE above it. The hard time does not have to define you. People are watching you. Not in a creepy, stalker way, although it can feel like it if you have ever tried to go to the bathroom or shower with small children in your house. In a way that allows them to pick up on your strength. So, to me, this year is a complete success.

I am loving day one of thirty-seven and I have no fear of thirty-eight and beyond if I just remember to *Be Still*. Let's not forget that some people don't get the opportunity to celebrate turning thirty-seven. I am grateful for it. Happy Birthday to me.

School Project Snub

You guys, my kids won't let me help them with school projects and I am NOT okay with that. I know...I know...

I was a teacher and I realize that kids need to be creative, independent and responsible. I understand my need for control is slightly depressing and seriously concerning. But, you guys, I create really great projects! Honestly, I was never a great test taker, but I kicked ass if there was a project option. I can be artistic, clever, resourceful and my ideas are BEYOND! Plus, I am old enough to use a glue gun and fabric scissors. All good projects need glue guns and fabric scissors! Yup. You can do so much more with a glue gun than a glue stick, thank you very much. Don't my kids understand this? I'm about to create my own Star Student poster just to fulfill the gap in my soul.

I didn't even mention that my house has become a hoarding ground for cardboard boxes that my son INSISTS are essential in our life. Because you just never know when you might want to build a cardboard castle or spaceship. Am I right?

Don't get me wrong, I am ALL for nurturing creativity and letting kids be messy, imaginative little people. But I can't even move around my family room or kitchen without knocking over a pile of boxes. The real kicker is that most of them are for Eddie's school STEM project (actually STREAM because they include art and religion- my STEM teacher friends will love that).

Most recently, he's been creating a Ski ball game out of recycled goods for a school carnival (not sure where the religion is there, but Lucy did create a boat for Jonah). Mind you, every Friday there is ONE child who walks out of school carrying a variety of boxes larger than his body, often with the assistance of his teacher. Wearing a smile and grass stains on his knees.

Just ONE child out of the whole school. EVERY Friday.

And on Friday's, that out-of-the-box thinker piles these boxes into my minivan and then into my living space. Five weeks now. NO END IN SIGHT! From these boxes, we have a ramp. A very large ramp. In my family room. I am sure it is only a matter of time until there are targets for the Ski balls. Any day now. I offer suggestions, modifications to his blueprint and I get dramatic eye rolls because I know nothing. No one can make you feel like more of an idiot than your own child. My knowledge and expertise are NOWHERE near that of a second grader. I remind him that I was on the teacher planning committee for a year before our district opened a 5-8 STEM building. I have a bachelor's degree from University of Dayton and a master's degree from THE Ohio State University. I say this to him as if any of it matters. He is not impressed. Whatever. That was back when I wore dress slacks and button up shirts. He does not know that person.

So, I will live amongst boxes. I will keep my problem solving and inspiring ideas to myself. I will let them be and develop their own creative genius. I will plop the glops of hot glue where they tell me and swallow my opinion when I know it is not the best spot.

But I will NOT be happy about it. Woe IS me. And if any adult family members want to make their own personal Star Student posters, I'm game.

When Does School Start?

I'd give my left arm to have time with my kids, but I'd give BOTH arms for them to be in school. Like, right now.

Yes, we are living amongst boxes.

Yes, we are in a new city.

Yes, it has rained EVERY day this week.

This may or may not explain why I sent both kids to their rooms with iPads so that I could paint my nails, drink my coffee and watch my Today Show. (I claim it as "mine" because we are a family, Hoda, Savanna, Al and me. And we need each other.)

I realize these are not real problems, but....
- I have NOT found Home Goods
- I have NOT discovered a close Marshals/TJ Maxx
 - I am a sucker for a routine

Life is hard, people. It is not all magic and memories. It is mostly yelling, deep breathing, and coffee. It contains constant google searches for an affordable area rug that costs less than my children's college fund. It requires patience in pursuing the perfect nightstand that will still allow you to pay the grocery bill.

It's hard and ugly and messy these days.

My little people, whom I love, have somehow become more winy and obnoxious in their tone and I cannot seem to undo it. I get actual goosebumps of disgust and anger when they ask me for another snack. Seriously! It's been 5 minutes. I know, it's disturbing. It appears to be acceptable behavior for them to slap the heck out of each other if one of their toes should touch the other person.

What has happened to us? How have we become such savages? Willing to risk the life of a loved one for the last potato chip! We've sunk very low, my little family.

Very low indeed. I blame summer. We yearn for the structure of our school routine and the outside world.

I fear that until August, this inhumane behavior will continue. We are actively contributing to the downward spiral of society. Hurry up, August. The fate of my family depends on you.

Magical Memory Myth

Awe...the Magical Memories.

Remember the days when you skipped through the apple farm, hand in hand, whistling along to "Doe a Deer?" When the children begged to be dressed in coordinated outfits? Perfectly suited for the cover of Good Housekeeping. And how everyone just loved getting their picture taken together in order to capture this magical moment- desperately wanting to hold hands, hug and kiss each other because there is just SO MUCH LOVE? Don't you remember these days?

Yeah. Me either.

I remember it being too hot or too cold. I can recall looking at my husband with pleading eyes. Eyes that screamed "these little people are out of control!" So many times, thinking, why can't we do this apple picking, magical thing? Everyone else seems to have it DOWN! What is wrong with us? I mean, do we even like each other because I don't like who we are when we do this? It was really more like a traveling circus on steroids. Frantic running, apple throwing, sporadic screaming, stick jousting, intensity.

We must be missing something! I remember kids whining, arguing over apples and feeling, at times, overwhelmingly frustrated. Luckily, without fail, we leave laughing. Knowing that our "magic" looks a lot more like chaos. What else can you really do? This is usually how we deal with our imperfections. Humor. Thank God for humor. We have a lot of humor simply because we have a lot of imperfections.

Pictures can be incredibly deceiving, don't you think? So, if you are headed out to the apple farm or pumpkin patch this weekend, excited for the magic that lies ahead, God speed. And if you discover Good Housekeeping type magic, good for you. Really, good for you.

But if, by chance, you don't find the magic please don't lose sleep over it. It's just not worth it. In the end the craziness will be an amazingly funny memory your family can look back on. For the rest of us, let's cling to humor and the hope that at least one shot will work for those magical holiday cards.

Cheers to humor and magical, slightly tainted memories.

Shaping the Spirited

Another snowy morning, another day full of possibilities and fighting about brushing teeth. More coffee, please. It's personal, and hard to admit, but I have a difficult child. (I feel like there should be a support group for moms like me.) The pediatrician refers to him as "spirited". However, you want to label it, an article I read today must have used him as their model.

Many of you either have, or know a child who:
- prefers to push the limits
- learns the hard way
- digs their heels when they feel they are right (frequently)
- goes full speed from morning to night

Many of you also know that these bouncy, little people are immediately seen as a behavior problem, having "issues", needing spanked, labeled ADHD, or lack discipline at home. I know this because I have been told all of these things, which is hard to admit. (Taking a deep breath now.) While, I have pursued all of these possibilities with both teachers and doctors, my child is simply "spirited." He is a MORE of everything.

"It's exhausting and maddening, no doubt, but there's also a beauty in their boldness." Mary Sheedy Kurcinka, *Raising Your Spirited Child.*

What is so wrong, after all, with having strong opinions? Why is society trying so hard to fit these kids into a box of obedience? Why can't we let them be little and active and maybe even, heaven forbid, wild? Where's the imagination? What are we so afraid of by letting kids act like kids?

Having been a teacher, I completely understand the pressure schools are under to have high performing students. We desperately need them to be obedient in order to complete the given tasks. For spirited kids, and many others, that's not so easy.

"Obedience is not their strong suit, but it isn't because they're deliberately trying to make us lose our shit, it's because they obey only when our request aligns with their opinions."
~Kurcinka

Although, I'm 99% confident that my son IS trying to get me to go to the dark side at times, this is really interesting. Am I teaching him that it's more important to obey than to trust his gut? (Yes, I know that there are times when they HAVE to obey in order to survive and function as a responsible human in society.) Where is the balance? Why is parenting so HARD?

The book also points out that, "*As difficult as it can be to raise a spirited kid, it's got to be even more difficult to be one.*" Oh. I never EVER thought about that. I'm likely to lose my "parent of the year" endorsement any day now. 'Parenting' magazine is calling me as type this. But that is such an interesting point!

He is constantly trying to navigate in a world where he wants to go full steam ahead, yet everywhere he turns is told he is "too much."

Slow down!

Take it easy!

Don't throw the ball that hard!

Don't run that fast!

Stop asking so many questions!

I have been so worried about him staying out of trouble and being accepted by his peers (and even me, as his mom, being accepted by other moms), that I was blind to the idea that he is told "you are too much" on a daily basis. How crushing. (I'm going to go cry in my closet for a few minutes.)

"Judgement can be strong when it comes to raising a dynamo."

Yup. Ugh, the judgement. That is the reason so many parents, myself included, often put our expectations on our children because of how others will view us as parents. Not, necessarily because it is right for the child.

Over the years, I have gotten much better about accepting him for who he is. Brushing off parent judgement knowing that my boy is doing tremendously well conquering this world. I'm less likely to be offended when he is not invited to parties, or when parents make comments. But, have you seen his smile? Or listened to him tell a story? Did you know that he cleans the snow off my car every morning before school? Have you seen him pitch a baseball? Or his intensity on the soccer field? You'd melt if you saw him push through his reading book knowing it's incredibly difficult for him. And when I had to take some really gross medication a few weeks ago he told me, "You can do this mom, you've done braver and harder things than this." Oh, Buddy. (Did you just sigh when you read that part? I did.)

My boy. Highest of highs and lowest of lows. But, still, mine.

"You haven't been cursed with a hard-to-manage kid, you've been entrusted to shape a powerful force."

YES! So, shape on, Mama's and Papa's. I realize that some days, that so-called 'powerful force' will IN FACT knock me on my ass or bring me to my knees. My advice? Load up on coffee first and say a few curse words under your breath. We need each other to shape these kids. Judge less. Support more.

Shape Away!

Monsters Have Taken Over

My children were replaced by monsters.

Holy Hell, guys. I don't know where my children went this weekend, but I'd like them back, please. Before you sent out search parties please know my children were physically here- in the flesh. However, whatever spirit invaded their little bodies was full of pure evil. Honestly, I'm not sure how my husband and I survived it.

Apparently, now we can argue and negotiate everything. I mean EVERYTHING. Also, if you don't want to do something, you just say "No." Like the old 1990s DARE program "Just Say No." My husband and I must have missed the parenting newsletter that deems this behavior of saying "no" and negotiating everything acceptable.

Whatever foreign creature that took over my small humans was INTENSE, aggressive and unable to understand typical human conversations. I'm guessing whoever was inside of them was used to a different form of communication. I suppose wherever that creature lives, it is necessary to argue and sigh using their whole body in order to survive. There must have been hours of practice put in to the depth in which their eyes can roll! I'll give this thing credit for standing its ground, however, its ground is stupid.

In this house, we generally encourage brushing teeth and hair, showering, flushing the toilet, NOT staring a screen for an unlimited time and putting the juice back in the fridge. We also appreciate a normal octave and volume of voice control. Although, we agree, it's impressive to be able to reach such high and low tones, it's also repulsively disrespectful.

I'm sure none of you know ANYTHING about this because, well, children are little blessings from above. Maybe you spent your weekend making magical memories at the pumpkin patch or picking apples and baking an adorable homemade pie. And most days, I would agree. But, based on the insanity I witnessed this weekend, today is not one of those days. So, how do you muster up the strength to NOT lose your damn mind? Who knows? I guess you just power through anxiously awaiting school on Monday.

Six months ago, I would have handled this invasion by losing my damn mind. There would have been lots of yelling, sarcasm and shame thrown right back at them. I would have forgotten to slow down, breath and take on one ridiculous situation at a time. I would have questioned everything about every parenting strategy I've ever tried and started googling counseling experts in the area. (I still question myself plenty! Just at a more realistic level.) My husband would have the biological aliens to deal with as well as talk his wife off a ledge. There would have no doubt been a full family breakdown where everyone was losing. No winners would be residing here.

How did I avoid that metaphorical "ledge" of despair? I kept my cool by reminding myself that it's all temporary. They won't go to high school without showering, right? Probably. Maybe. Also, a grateful heart really does wonders for staying calm in crisis. I knew my kids had a good situation going for them. They have a family that will not tolerate this behavior, and, in the end, they will be okay. If I lose my temper, I will be disappointed with myself. Currently, I only need to be disappointed with my kids. (Side note- I lose my cool PLENTY. I yell PLENTY. And I'm learning that it doesn't really work and just makes me feel angry.)

And when I'm reading things like *"Who we are and how we engage with the world are much stronger predictors of how our children will do than what we know about parenting,"* from people I admire (Brené Brown), it pushes me to be better. When she's asking questions like *"Are you the adult that you want your child to grow up to be?"* I can say, yes. Most of the time I am. But when I lose my temper or shame my kids, that's NOT the kind of person I want them to be. Finally, I knew I had back-up. I was not alone. Teammates are the best.

Listen, you guys know that raising children is no joke. Some days are about survival and other days are magic pumpkins and fairytale hay rides. I get it. Anyone who knows me understands that I am in the thick of it with you. My children toe the line of blissful parenting and little monsters very well. But every day, we all wake up and try again. Guess what? The kids are going to be okay you guys, they are going to be just fine. Stop stressing about all the details and just be good humans to them. They will catch on…eventually.

Someone asked how my weekend was and I replied, "It was great." Because I was still able to enjoy my weekend with my husband without feeling all angry and agitated about it. I'm sure my kids would tell you it was terrible without TV or technology. However, we played some killer card games and built a sweet Lego set until the demons slowly exited their bodies.

We can do hard things. We can even do them without losing our damn minds. Most of the time, anyway.

There's Room for All of Us

I was home over the holiday break and catching up with some of my most favorite people. You know, the ones that you keep in your back pocket for rainy days. The ones that remind you of some of the happiest, most ridiculous days you lived. The ones that love you even though they witnessed those ridiculous days. Yup, those people.

Instead of sharing our profound thoughts about fashion trends or the latest celebrity drama, we were talking about parenting. Because we are grown-ups. And we are mothers for GOODNESS SAKE!

I was explaining to them how each night at bedtime I ask my daughter to tell me one thing that made her happy and one thing that made her sad that day. I started to tell them how I do this each day and then immediately started choking on my words. Mind you, I was not eating anything, but I was full of "it".

I stopped myself and said, "What in the hell am I talking about? I do NOT do this every night! That's ridiculous! Who am I kidding?" Do I use this strategy with my kids? Absolutely. Is it a nightly occurrence where we all hold hands and talk about our days? No.

And my lovely friends and I all burst out in honest laughter. God bless their sweetness for actually believing I was capable of being some type of Mother Goddess. Let's just take a break right there. Yes, I have had this conversation with my kids. But MOST nights? Let's be real please.

MOST nights I do a tip-toe victory dance out of her room and skip to my bed like a scene from a Broadway musical. Jazz hands and all. Wearing my favorite glamorous Pelotonia t-shirt, I binge watch BRAVO or tear through the pages of my current book. Those BRAVO ladies do make me feel better about myself while simultaneously worry about the values in this country.

How's that for Motherhood Goddess? BAM!

Now, some of you have these adorable conversations with your children each night. If you do, I think that's awesome. I think you should feel good about yourself and what you do for your kids. Those bedtime routines make lasting memories for your kids. Even the ones that are less than perfect. Sharing, loving, laughing and goodnight squeezes make the world go around. If you have the energy to bring that magic each night, be confident that you have that skill down.

You Do You!

But, it's just NOT me. At least, it's not routinely me. And I'm SO OKAY with that! We can all still be Motherhood Goddesses. There is room for all of us!

Let the Boy Sweep

Just another Tuesday pick-up from our sweet little school. The sun was a little bit shinning and the clouds were a little bit grim, teasing the possibility of rain. (Or maybe snow. It is Northeast Ohio after-all.) Right on cue and a few minutes early, out runs my third grader, just slightly before the rest of his class which always leaves me puzzled. But, arguably, by the time I ask why he is first again, the rest of his class comes pouncing out the door. A bunch of half crazed animals on the edge of scape!

First words from my boy, "Mom, I got to sweep the whole classroom today!" Choking on my own laughter, I took a breath.

I know what you're thinking because it's probably what I was thinking. What 3rd grader WANTS to sweep the whole classroom? Why would a little boy OBSESSED with sports, competition and a bit self-conscience make this choice and be happy about it? Right? It just does not add up. There must be more to this spell-binding story.

With legitimate excitement beaming from his eyes, I realized I needed to handle this one carefully to get the full story. Very carefully. As parents, you know when to tread lightly in order to get the goods. One false move, and I'd lose him and his confidence in me.

I don't want my son to assume I don't believe him. But too often I doubt him. It's kind of terrible that I didn't just trust that maybe, MY boy was a little precious after-all. But, I didn't.

So, like an animal stalking its prey, I moved in slowly.

"Really? Tell me more about that." Says this curious mother. If I've learned anything about childhood psychology, it's not to attack. Try to get them to volunteer the information.

As his story hopped around from, "I just wanted to…well the janitor…my shoes were dirty from recess…I was only going to do mine, but then I did the whole class," etc. The story was "iffy" at best and constantly changing like my nail polish color. For sure, something fishy was going on. It just didn't add up. Yet, he kept insisting that he wanted to sweep!

I asked a little buddy of his standing next to us in the pick-up line if anything exciting led to my son deciding to become master sweeper. And the poor kid just looked up at me all wide-eyed, "*Um, well, I'm not sure. He did? Maybe I wasn't in the room. Yea, that's it. I must have been in the bathroom.*" That's not much of an alibi. After that storms of stutters, I let that sweet kid off the hook. If he was protecting his friend, I certainly was not going to be the one to get in the way of that.

Deep breath. Let it go. If there was something that serious, the school would have gotten in touch with me. I would have gotten a phone call or email if they wanted me involved. I'll be sure to check any missed calls or emails when I get home. But, for that moment, I needed to carry on with the afternoon and not obsess over it. Maybe, just maybe I didn't need to know everything that happened at school.

I let it go the whole afternoon while we fought our way through spelling words and subject and predicate homework. I let it go during free time when I caught up with Ellen. I let it go while I prepped dinner. But when my husband walked in, I did not let it go. I dished the whole scenario in a whispered hush knowing that he would share in my suspicions. He laughed and shook his head while the little sweeper man walked into the kitchen.

Within seconds he was all over the poor kid. Using the same calm, curious questioning I had used. "Did you make a mess with your muddy shoes and have to clean it up?" and "Buddy, it's not a big deal. We are happy you did your part. We just want to understand WHY you swept the whole classroom?"

And all the kid could come up with was "I just wanted to sweep!". Nothing more. We both exhaled deeply and agreed to let it be. It is what it is.

A few days later I emailed about an electric gradebook password question and casually mentioned the sweeping incident. (I know. I didn't really let it go, I guess. I'm just the worst sometimes.) Among other sweet compliments, this is what his teacher wrote: "*About him sweeping the classroom, it's one of the classroom jobs. Eddie seems to really like this job, no matter who is assigned the job he asks if he can do it!*"

You guys. That's it. That's the truth. There's no more to the story. He just really likes to sweep. I spent the afternoon and evening interrogating a completely innocent kid. I assumed the worst. I was 100% wrong. Ahh, parenting. I just can't seem to get it right!

That boy just wanted to sweep, and I should have trusted him. I'm his mom.

"I was so busy trying to raise a good kid that I didn't realize I already had one." ~Glennon Doyle.

Yup. I should have listened to that advice. Turns out I have a pretty good kid. Maybe, just maybe, he's a little precious after-all. He must get that from his father.

Toothpaste Trauma

I've found it. The thing that will end me. The one act that will drive me to the nut house. White jacket. Heavily medicated and drooling. The image locked forever in my brain causing my eyes to roll back in my head as I slur incoherently.

Do you know the paste-like, neon toothpaste cemented to my kid's bathroom sink?

That's it. That's all it takes, folks.

Don't roll your eyes. The actual site of the sink brings a sense of anger that doubles my blood pressure. Goosebumps worthy. If you're a parent, then you've likely lived with this same version of hell! Am I right? The struggle is real, and I can't keep quiet anymore. I can tell what they had for breakfast just by looking in the sink. That's ridiculous. No one should see that.

And why SO much toothpaste? If you have a little mouth, you only need a little toothpaste! It's not a genius level activity this tooth brushing thing. Yes, I've taught them how to brush. Yes, I've given repeated lessons on how to spit. Obviously, I've given them demos on how to rinse their sink. Yet- STILL! Still I find chunks of gooey paste glued to the porcelain sink and newly upgraded zodiac countertops. I've had them clean it in attempt to prevent the fatal paste spillage. No go.

This is parenthood. Scraping goop off of surfaces with the same utensil I use to clean crunchy bits off of a cast iron skillet. These are the desperate details no one tells you about, guys. "Have kids!" they say. "Treasure every moment," I've heard. So many details conveniently left out in the books and pep talks.

Parenthood. The magic and mayhem.

So, for those of you with tiny people (younger than six and eight) train them early! Rinse that sink like your life depends on it. These are LIFE LONG lessons! Their roommates will thank them. Their future spouses will thank them. But mostly, you will thank yourself. These lessons are the secret to success. I hope that all of you miss out on sink scraping, mind boggling, ridiculousness.

As for me, I'll be in one bathroom or another cursing the combination of hardened toothpaste and porcelain.

Sign-Up Genius Spiel

You know what I just realized last week? You don't have to sign-up for everything! You really don't. Maybe I'm a little late to this reckoning, but I've made it now. The world keeps right on spinning on its dysfunctional axis whether or not I sign up for things at school. Promise.

I do, however, have to remind myself that I don't have to be everything to everybody else. I just have to be everything to myself. Let's be kind and gentle with ourselves for a bit.

Going back to made up social media holidays, please add 'National Sign-Up Genius Day' to the list. If you're not familiar with Sign-Up Genius, it's actually a super easy way to organize and get volunteers for school parties and other things. If you are a room parent; it's a life saver! (Side note- Gold bless all the room moms/dads/people out there. That job is NO joke! You've got my respect and appreciation.)

So, the day the official Sign-Up Genius email makes it to your inbox is like the Black Friday of parenthood. If your heart is set on a fall harvest snack, drink or paper products- you better get your click on quick. Otherwise, you will get left organizing a class craft, game or goodie bag. If you're really not on the ball, you might get left with- hold your breath- NOTHING! You could risk getting shut out of all-party festivities. Everything. And then your children might not remember that you love them! (Please tell me you can hear my sarcasm on that last line!)

How will you get 'Parent of the Year' if you don't put together the most adorable holiday themed goodie bags, though? Oh, the shame!

(Also, side note- Do America's children honestly need more goodie bags? Don't you think it's possible we've overdone it on the goodie bags? Do we really need more plastic in our homes in order to create a magical childhood? Is it wise to blow forty bucks on junk the kids only care about for one day? Um, no. So much NO!)

154

Anyway, I was slightly delayed logging into my sign-up. (By "slightly," I mean 7seven hours after it went out because I was sleeping. I know. What was I thinking?) Guess what? My favorite categories, drinks and paper products, were already gone. Damn. I did start to get a little panicky that I wouldn't get to help with the parties. But then I stopped myself.

Wait. Hold your horses, Angie. Pick one or two parties that you can kick ass at and be done.

I actually got that idea from Rachel Hollis author of "Girl, Wash your Face." She encourages us to focus on keeping it simple. Pick what you like, the ONE thing, kick ass at it and move on. So, I listened to my pal, Rach, and did exactly that.

You know what's great about only choosing one or two things for the whole year? There's a whole army of parents excited about clicking on their one or two things. At my school, there is no shortage of helpful, loving moms, dads, and grandparents. Everything will be covered. The children will not have to face the Fall Harvest without pumpkin plates. Whew. (Please know I am well aware many schools are NOT like this. Trust me I get it. I have taught in those schools.)

Some moms really want to bake cupcakes with those spider rings, or mummy shaped cake-pops. There are precious parents out there who honestly enjoy putting those goodie bags together. Let them! Neither of those options are my jam and that's okay. My jam is juice boxes and appropriately themed napkins from Home Goods. I will kick ass at the paper product game, you guys.

At the same time, if I do not provide pumpkin plates or help work the fall festival, the hearts of my children will not stop beating. They will breath just the same if Hudson's mom (who took the day off work to be with her son) runs the pumpkin decorating station. My children will still laugh, make memories and down too much sugar. It's a fact, jack.

They will go to the party loved.
They will come home loved.
Amen.

We are a village and we come together for the sake of the goodie bags and magical memories. Don't get carried away thinking it's all up to you to create these memories. It's not. You've got all of us.

Calm Like a Cucumber

This is a constant go-to quote for me because it can be applied in so many situations.

"We can do hard things." ~ Glennon Doyle

It's simple yet holds so much value to our lives. It's a gentle remind that life is hard and that's perfectly okay. Living through difficult times does not have to be a game changer. When I say, "hard things", I could be referring to dealing with hair loss, arthritis or other autoimmune issues. We all deal with our own "hard things" like personal demons, body image issues, relationships, finances, etc.

Whatever. What I am ACTUALLY referring to as the hardest of things is surviving the summer with my kids. These are HARD THINGS! The rest I can manage.

I did many hard things today:

- I got them to do their chores before ten am. Even if I had to slowly sip and swallow my lukewarm coffee while they huffed and puffed like two of the three little pigs.

- I took them to the grocery store for two items I forgot yesterday. AND I calmly, asked Eddie to put back the four bags of chocolate chips he snuck in the basket, and kindly asked Lucy to re-stack the fifteen water bottles she knocked over. I was so well behaved, you guys. Calm like a cucumber even if I was boiling on the inside.

- At lunch, when my adorably clumsy daughter spilled a whole cup of blueberry juice on my neutral fabric colored bar stools- the neighbors may have heard my immediate reaction with the windows shut. But then I regrouped. I reminded myself that we can do hard things. Like clean up juice stains with minor grumbling under

my breath about how I should have gotten a dark grey fabric instead. (But the island cabinet is grey, and I was worried it would be too much.) I pushed on. I survived it. Even when she went to put her hands in the pockets of her romper and realized it was on backwards.

- I also knew I could do hard things when I offered to make cookies for my son's team dinner. Homemade? Sure! Baseball shape? You bet! With that glossy icing? Well, absolutely! (Mind you, no one asked me these questions. I just really like to push myself in my ability to do hard things!) And when my kids made some too thin and some too thick, I had to talk my controlling personality off the ledge. "These are for kids. Baseball boys WILL eat anything. They eat dirt and sunflower seeds. No pressure." I said to no one in particular.

And so...they are now playing outside. This is another way I set myself up for hard things. Because we all know how long happy siblings play together. I'm sure they are holding hands and singing Kumbaya as I type!

I know all of you are out there doing these kinds of hard things, too. Working parents and stay-home parents, the end of summer can make you rethink it all! Pat yourselves on the back. These kids are tricky business and we are all doing it anyway.

God Speed and God Bless. Warriors- all of you. Survivors in my book.

Bless the Coaches

"Your boy, he has FIRE in his eyes!"

Says the new soccer coach with a thick Eastern European accent.

Yup. Nailed it. I don't have to tell most of you about this fire.

The last week has been designated 'Teacher and Nurse Appreciation Week.' Many of you have graciously been doing kind acts to thank nurses and teachers. (Who, by the way are some of my most favorite people and the BEST professions you can choose.) However, I'd also like to take a sec and thank all those coaches out there. The good ones are so often forgotten, aren't they?

These coaches work tirelessly and thanklessly with little or no pay. Usually volunteers that CHOOSE to spend time developing our big and little people simply because they have a passion for it.

I'll never forget our first soccer practice in California when my son's new coach walked up in a Block "O" t-shirt (first sign of a good human who also happens to be a fan of The Ohio State University) and introduced himself to us. Being only a kindergartner in a new city, seeing signs of home was an immediate comfort for both of us. It was an intense season of skill and drill two-hour practices twice a week and my son was all in. After the first game where he ran his heart out and left everything on that field, the coach grabbed him.

"You've got insane intensity. We are going to find a way to celebrate that intensity." Rich Coury

Um, what? A kid who was constantly told to settle down, simmer, relax, take a breath- was told to CELEBRATE it? Can we just celebrate you, Coach Rich? And he did. Every game. Every practice. He never settled for less than full speed from my guy. And my boy soaked it up. Turned it on. Never backed down. Felt safe and successful being 100% himself.

This is what our coaches do. They see the best (or beast) our kids have to offer and CELEBRATE it. It gives permission for boys and girls, like Eddie, to go full speed while instilling respect, discipline and love for the sport.

He gave my son permission to be himself.

I've tried to slow him down, but the truth is sports are SUCH a great escape for him and it has everything to do with tremendous coaching relationships. So, please- CELEBRATE the coaches in your life. Let them know they matter and it's worth all the time they dedicate to the sport and the kids. (And maybe a special prayer for coach's significant others!)

Find people that let your spirited kids keep that fire in their eyes.

This Is the Hard Stuff

I am strong. I can handle most anything that life throws at me. Most anything, that is. I realize (and science confirms) that I am resilient and strong due to my struggles. The challenges that have tested me over the years have proven to be opportunities to grow stronger, more hopeful. My brain is trained to think hopeful thoughts because of adversity. At this phase of life, I'm grateful for my adversity.

I can handle most anything life throws at me. Once again, most anything. With each passing year, hell, each passing day, I'm discovering that watching my children struggle is excruciating.   EXCRUCIATING. Like, in all caps! Give me the weight of the world, the learning and social struggles. Pile it on me like my never-ending laundry. I can take it. I can take the pain, the insecurity, the worries. Oh, all the worries they have. But do NOT make me stand by and watch them struggle through it. I'm not sure I'm strong enough for that.

I know. I know. The struggle is what builds strength and forms who we are. TRUST me- I get it. I will write page after page about how my imperfections and misdirection's have completely made me the person I am. BUUUUUT, how am I supposed to stand by and be a witness? Ugh. The horror! Even my dear friend and researcher (who I've never met and does not know I exist.) Yet, Brené Brown says,

"Children with high levels of hopefulness have experience with adversity. They've been given the opportunity to struggle and in doing that they learn how to believe in themselves."
Daring Greatly

Meaning, I'm going to have to stand by and watch them be uncomfortable, be disappointed, heartbroken and even fail. You know, I didn't realize I was signing up for all of this. I have to see it in their eyes, feel it in their little sighs. I can squeeze them a little tighter, tell them I love them and be ready to scoop the ice cream. I will have the hard, uncomfortable conversations, run the tight ship and remind them that they are "enough." But I cannot let them miss the struggle. It's part of life, maybe even the most important part and I hate it.

I want them to learn, grow and most importantly, believe in themselves. There's nothing more important to me than that. But, as a parent, watching the struggle is SO much harder than living the struggle.

I'm not writing because I have great advice to share. I don't even have a "You Got This" kind of message. In fact, quite the opposite. Life is hard. Parenting is harder. Some days I've "got" this, but today is not that day. Today I worry, pray, have a little faith and a lot of hope. I suppose, ironically, it's my adversity that's given me this hope. According to the professionals, anyway. It's not fair that love goes so hand-in-hand with worry. Or that hope comes from adversity.

So, I will hope that one day my kids will reflect on their childhood and be grateful for their challenges knowing that it made them better humans in the long run. Here's looking at you kid. Better yet, here's looking at you PARENTS. This is the hard stuff.

I'm going to need some more coffee.

Your Kid May Not Be Who You Were Hoping For

That's a tough pill to swallow. But guess what? You can feel this way and STILL love them with every inch of your being. You CAN feel both and still be a great parent.

Although attending a traditional Catholic mass is not new to my family, they had attended public school until our recent move to Cleveland, Ohio. The kids will be attending sweet, small Catholic school in our new town which includes mass every Tuesday morning. My daughter enjoys the songs, being with friends and the lessons she picks up at mass. However, my son has a particularly difficult time with the routine of a Catholic mass. (He claims there is too much sitting, standing and listening. Followed by more sitting, standing and listening. Shockingly there are no stage performers to keep his attention.)

Families are always welcome to join the students for Tuesday mass. I walk into church, already protecting my heart, knowing this may be a stressful hour for both of us. I desperately want him to make a good impression with the new families and friends who are surrounding him. And yes, I do realize that I worry too much and often expect the worst when I could just give him the benefit of the doubt.

"Worry less," they say.

"He will find his way," people tell me.

Even the pediatrician told me last week, "*You do too much. I give you permission to take a step back.*" Seriously. The struggle between "helicopter mom" and "free-range parent" is INTENSE. So anyway, with my head low, peeking between the pews looking for his class, I spot him. Before mass has even started, he is seated in-between the wall and the teacher. No kids sitting around him. Hmm. Interesting.

This is not a positive reflection of his church behavior. My heart sinks to my toes and I release a deep sigh. There it is. He is the student that needs moved away from his buddies. No matter how I over or under parent him. He is who he is. Learning the hard way, is exactly how he learns, and I need to let him.

And I can be sad. I can sit around and mourn the easy-going, rule following little man I always imagined I would have. And I do.

After mass, I sit in my car and give myself the five-minute drive home to drop a few tears for that little man that does not exists. But then, I get home and see his baseball shoes, and soccer shoes, and the blanket he still snuggles and all I've got left is love. I have to remind myself that it's not about me. Parenting is not about the expectation other parents have for me or my children. It's about letting him learn and loving him through it. Forget the looks or the reputation he may or may not get. That's not my role and honestly, it's pretty selfish of me to mold a kid that makes me look good. It's not about us. It's about the kids. Let them flounder. Let them get in trouble. Let them be a little bit more of everything.

To the parents whose little people get moved in church. For those parents who get notes and emails of concern from teachers. Your child may not be the person you imagined.

In fact, they are simply MORE than you imagined.
MORE struggle and MORE strength.
MORE tears and more laughs.
MORE intensity in every way leaving room for more love and success in the end.

I feel you. It's okay to admit this about your children without discounting your love for them. You can feel BOTH. Just try not to choke when you swallow that reality pill. They may not be who you were hoping for because they may actually be even better.

Chapter Seven: Growing Bold and Bald with Alopecia Areata

"Write Hard and Clear About What Hurts."
~Ernest Hemingway

This one is hard. This one hurts. And, to be honest, this one is embarrassing. I am bearing it all, including my increasingly bald head and it sucks. I wish there was a more glamorous word than that, but it's the most accurate.

After another exciting round of GI testing, I was diagnosed with a microscopic form of Colitis known as Lymphocytic Colitis. Believe it or not, this is much better news than the Ulcerative Colitis I was given in the past because it is CURABLE! Words I don't hear often enough. It does mean a new steroid for twelve weeks, which is annoying. However, if it rids me of this form of Colitis, it is a HUGE win! HUGE - name the movie! I've been through a million and seven med changes over the years so this 'aint no big thang.

On spring break, my family noticed a golf ball size bald spot behind my left ear. It was alarming and shocking for me. I had noticed increase hair loss in the shower, yet, steroids typically give me thinning hair. Also, there were no alarming large handfuls of hair loss at this point, but plenty of thinning over the years. Thinning. Never bald spots.

Over the last few weeks, there may have been some developments within my autoimmune system. And not, necessarily in the direction I was hoping. I've tried to live in denial (which is just such a happy place to be, am I right?) and downplay the recent and rapid increase of the hair loss. Then I found the spot on the top of my head. Damn. Here we go.

After calling the doctor in hopes that it was a side effect of the new steroid, she told me this was the medication option with the LEAST amount of side effects. Less than 5% of people on this med experience hair thinning/loss. (Once again, LUCKY ME! - I am so undeniably special that I fit into that itsy-bitsy percentage.) She was willing to decrease the timing from twelve weeks to nine. Changing meds would likely decrease the success of my GI recovery.

So, here's a question for you. Would you like to eat food like normal people, or have a full head of hair?

I totally understand that some of you would say "STOP the meds!" But the condition I was living in with colitis was life changing. Feeling nauseous, drained and depleted altered the way I lived my life. I have family and friends with incurable forms of Colitis/Crones, and I know they would do anything to kick its ass out of their body. I had to dig down, like below sea level kind of down, where those strange looking sea creatures live, and accept the risk of more hair loss. I had to grab on to some sort of strength.

So, I thought about what matters to me most: family, friends, faith and health.

- Is my husband going to love me less? (Quite the opposite, he constantly reminds me how cute I am in hats.)

- Will my kids think less of me?

- What if my friends are embarrassed to be with me? (No more than they are with a full head of hair!)

- Will my family feel sorry for me? (More likely to share my anger. One reaction was "damn," not pity.)

- Is it enough to shake my faith? (Probably the most ridiculous question.)

- Does this interrupt my daily health journey? (Curing Colitis will drastically improve my way of life.)

After contemplating the most important aspects of my life and how they relate to hair loss, I had a "come to Jesus" moment. The things that matter most (family, friends, faith and health) cannot be taken away from me.

Ever.

I repeat, the very things that matter most can NOT be taken away from me.

I heard something like this when I listened to Glennon Doyle speak a few years ago in Upper Arlington, Ohio and haven't really needed it until now. Any illness or medication can NOT take away the very things that matter most.

That's heavy stuff, friends.

Although I'm not ready to talk about it, writing about it is my therapy. Once it's written, it becomes real and accepted. And then, I can move on to healing. Accept the shit storm of life and move the hell on.

For now, if you see me styling constant ponytails, or sporting adorable hats, just tell me how cute I look. No pity please. Pity makes me sad and I don't have time for that puddle. I still have SO much more good than bad in my life. So much more.

Side Note: I am at the Cleveland Clinic again for round two of my infusion and surrounded my favorite privacy curtain ready to watch *The Greatest Showman*. Coffee and snacks are on my trey table and my happy place is in full effect. (Honest-to-goodness guys, this privacy curtain is the things dreams are made of. I bet unicorns invented them.) I might do some online shopping for an Indians hat while I'm here, however, I have a freakishly small head making online shopping a little tricky. Youth hats, here I come!

Diagnosis Confirmed: Alopecia Areata

As my hair loss continued to increase, a fear swept in that it was not related to my steroid changes after all. That it may be a sign of something more serious and permanent. It was time to call for reinforcements. After working with both an endocrinologist and a dermatologist at the Cleveland Clinic, they confirmed that the hair loss is NOT related to medication, but in fact a deeper issue. The pattern and intensity of hair loss combined with 4 million blood tests ruled out a hormonal imbalance and confirmed Alopecia Areata.

Facts:
- Alopecia Areata is patchy hair loss on the head (different from whole body hair loss and kind of bullshit because I still have to shave my legs!)
- An autoimmune disease that I in NO way caused. My body is confused (as is my head) and thinks my hair follicles are "bad" therefore fighting them off. Experts do believe it is "triggered" by a stressful even although you are previously disposed to it.
- Once you are diagnosed with one autoimmune disease, especially in childhood, you are likely to be diagnosed with more. (I'm literally in 2% of the population.)
- There is NO cure. (Shocker!)
- I have lost half my hair and will likely lose more if not all.
- Treatments do have positive results and there are options, but chances of reoccurrence are also likely.
- Stress has been linked as a factor, although genetics and other unknown causes are the highest factor. (As my parents all say, "If stress was the main factor EVERYONE would be bald".)

Plan:

- Started a prescription foam applied to my head twice a day.
- Also bringing back the coolness of Rogaine by applying once a day.
- Waiting on insurance approval to start site steroid injections which will occur every four to six weeks. (The doc warned me about the pain associated with these, but I assured her that pain does not scare me. I've seen pain. Survived it. Bring it on.)
- Also recommended more "Me time," yoga and meditation. She put a heavy focus on being mindful and in touch with my emotions. Go for walks, slow down and focus on healing form the inside out. So, I'm sure my kids being home for the summer will be a GREAT stress reliever!

There you have it, folks. Onward and upward.

Not the news I was hoping for, but always aware that someone down the hall was getting a skin cancer diagnosis on the same day. You could say I'm scared out of my mind. You could say I'm pissed off. You would be right about both.

Trying to remain calm and optimistic, which is kind of like keeping your cool while the house is burning down around you. Oh look- there goes the kitchen. OOMMMMMMM. And the couch...and the bedroom. Namaste, friends.

You've Got This, We've Got You

What do you say when "Thank You" is not enough?

Are there words or actions more meaningful or powerful than that?

Have you ever been overwhelmed with gratitude? To the point where you push it out of your head because it is too much. The kind of feelings that actually fill your toes to your eye balls and you have to walk out of a room? Those feelings that burn the back of your eyes and make it hard to breath? Tell me you've felt that way before. It's just too much for me to vocalize. I can't seem to find the right words without becoming a puddle of mush. The feelings creep up and I push them away not knowing what to do with them.

The amount of love, sarcasm and overall support I've gotten over the last few weeks after sharing my diagnosis has caused a simultaneous heart/brain explosion. Texts, calls, hats, flowers, personal notes and more have flooded my home and my heart. It's too much. But, it's also everything. It matters. It matters so much and fuels my fire.

My husband, who has talked me off the ledge when I froze in fear of the clogged shower drain. I called him mid-day at work unable to speak. It was beyond cat-got-your-tongue kind of speechlessness. It was a powerful punch in the gut reminder of the unfairness of this disease. He could hear me hyperventilating into the phone attempting to understand why I was lying on the bathroom floor crying. I tried to spit out how the hair just kept coming through the drain, like a never-ending vine when I was cleaning it out. It just kept coming leaving my stomach in knots and tears collecting on the tile floor. Helpless and hopeless wrapped in a towel with a fist full of hair. Ugh.

But then, a new friend literally offered to shave her head, should things go there- Ugh. A new navy-blue hat saying "home" from a gentle, generous beauty that I'm lucky to call family and friend. Ugh. Another one from an old friend with the words "Force of Nature" stitched into it as a reminder of my own strength. Ugh.

And still another hand-crocheted by a lovely, talented friend arriving at my door within days of hearing the news. Ugh. It's too much and makes me feel like the luckiest girl in the world, despite my situation.

These gestures have allowed me to bounce back and see the good. Little reminders that you can, in fact, choose happiness.

And then there was yesterday afternoon. I discovered new spots and an increase in size of the old ones. The disease was progressing as expected. Despite lowering my meds, the hair issue has not slowed. You can imagine how that felt.

Accept it. Fix the ponytail and fix dinner. Go do life.

Within minutes, my husband handed me a package in the mail. As usual, I had temporary online shopping amnesia. Hmmm? What did I order last week? Did I? I don't think I did? Maybe I did? (This is a problem that results in an exciting surprise! Anyone else do this?) I opened it and immediately walked out of the room leaving the kids wondering in suspense. Both of them asking, what happened to Mama? Heartfelt concern as they saw my eyes welling up as fast as I exited the kitchen. A tsunami wave of feelings. Stopping my breath. Breaking me and healing me all at once.

It came at the right time. From the right people. A gift that left me surprised yet didn't surprise me at all. The unwavering love of your family. The people who have been my biggest supporters and cheerleaders since 1979.

A reminder of the only thing that matters. Love. A silver bracelet with the words **You've got this. We've got you,** engraved. It was signed generically from my cousins. Not one in particular, just all of them. I mean, I CAN'T EVEN with this one. Can't even deal. They do have me. With or without hair, their love of and for me remains the same. Meant to be worn as a constant reminder of support even on the days that make me question everything.

It will forever be my favorite thing. I would choose my family over sunsets, coffee and wine. Which is really saying something. Thank you all for "having" me, "getting" me, but mostly, for loving me. It's too much and it's everything. Thank you.

Love for Nurses

So, a nurse walks into a patient's room and says, "Do you know what's causing the hair loss?" My body language: head tilted down, eyes looking up at her with a snarky glimmer.

Me (out loud): "No. I was hoping you guys could help me with that." Smile, Angie, smile and be kind. Less smart ass and more compassion never hurt anybody.

Me (in my head): *Really? Seriously? Is there a hidden camera? If I knew WHY my hair was falling out, don't you think I would go ahead and FIX it? Like, oh, you know I think I had an allergic reaction to an apple and all my hair fell out. Maybe I should stop eating them? Thanks so much!*

Nurse: "Okay then. Have you had any stressful events recently in your life?"

Me (out loud): "Nothing out of the norm. I try to take good care of myself, I practice a healthy life style and live as balanced as I can."

Me (in my head): *Um yeah. You know what's stressful? When all of your hair starts falling out. That's been a pretty traumatic event. Does that count? I'm stressed about that one.*

Thank goodness for "in my head thoughts." They keep me sane and make me laugh, but for the nurse's sake, I'm also thankful for my filter to know the difference. (Disclaimer- the nurse was only asking the required questions and went on to inject the shots in my head as delicately as possible. I love nurses.)

Holy Shots

Holy Shit.

Pain. You know, the holy shit kind of pain? Intense. Finger gripping, leg shaking, kind of pain. Nothing emotional. All physical. No better way to describe it than Holy Shit.

I've seen pain. I've had pain. I've survived pain.

I was headed into the dermatologist prepared for my first round of steroid injections. I knew they would be in my scalp with the hopes of firing up some of those hair follicles to get them growing. The scheduling nurse had assumed it would be eight to ten injections and last around thirty minutes. Given the fact that it was a short appointment and my kids were on summer vacation, I brought them along. We headed out the appointment armed with I-Pads, crafts and snacks. No biggie. We've had to do this sort of thing before. When you are a parent, there are just times when your kids have to come with you to important appointments. That's just par for the parenting course.

Driving there, I asked the kids what they do when they are a little bit nervous. Because I was more than a smidge apprehensive. My daughter reminded me, "Mom, remember what you tell me? You can't be brave without being a little bit scared. Otherwise it would be easy. Just think of your happy place!" Excellent advice. It's nice to know someone is listening to me.

My son, "I don't know, mom. I've never been scared or had pain." Classic. Thanks, Bud. This kid. Must be nice to live in your world, little man.

Then I asked them what a good happy place would be. My husband can always tell when I'm nervous or scared by the way I keep the conversation flowing. I hate the stillness and silence of fear. So, I will fill it with random conversation, weird questions and anything to distract my head. My little lady excitedly suggested to think about the beach or the mountains. Very accurate as far as happy places go.

The little man, "Mom, remember when we went to look at puppies and they all were climbing all over us and we couldn't stop laughing?" And I did. A few weeks before we had gone to look at a litter of six-week-old Goldendoodles after losing our fourteen-year-old chocolate lab. The feeling of those furry bundles of love climbing all over you, my husband and kids all on the floor with me laughing. Oh, man. Freeze that feeling.

Yup. That's a good one. Puppies. I'll go with that. (Sometimes these kids are quite incredible.)

We arrived, got checked in quickly and kids happily zoned out (one of the times I feel technology is a gift!). The nurse walked in with one syringe, took one look at the lack of hair and said "Oh, you're going to need to wait on the doctor. This will not be enough." Apparently, the rapid progression of the hair loss was even alarming for her. And since the doctor has to prescribe the amount of steroid injections, she would need to reevaluate my head.

Crap. Now, I love my dermatologist. Her name is Angela Kyei and people travel across the country to come to her, which is why she is double booked and hard to get in to. God Bless the Cleveland Clinic.

So, we waited...and waited. An hour later, she came in and said and did one thousand things she did not have time for. I know I was not on her schedule. I know she was probably missing lunch. I know she cared as much as I did.

Basically, she told me:
- *This is going to be hard on you. Really hard.*
- *Your hair will likely keep falling out.*
- *This will hurt mentally and physically. You are going to have to dig deep.*
- *Treatment may not work at all.*
- *I am in this with you for the long haul. (And she is.)*

I think she thought that would scare me or sadden me. She didn't.

Some struggles in life, you can do everything right. You fight with everything you have. And then, you have to let it go.

Meaning that the sooner I accept this disease as part of me, the sooner I can get on with healing. Ok. I get it. I'm not there, yet. But I get it.

Nurse comes back with not one, but FOUR freaking syringes. I ask if she has ever taken on this big of a project before. And funny enough, she has not. She has never needed more than one, or two. Looks like she was doing something new today, too.

Sweet. Someone to take on a new challenge with me.

And we began. Now, pick your favorite bad word. Like, really bad word. This is not the time for daggnabit or shiitake mushrooms. Got one? I was digging deep and using my best yoga breathing techniques, toes curling under and fingernails digging into my thighs. I am sure I sounded like a bull getting ready for the races with the intensity of my throaty exhale. In... two...three...out...two...three.

I had to stop and take one break. I felt the tears burning. It was too much, and I needed to reset. While my daughter stayed totally occupied with her game behind the curtain, my sons' curious eyes were creeping. After he exclaimed that my head was dripping in blood, I calmly reassured him that I was fine and challenged him to get a new record on his game. I was struggling to push through at that point. But then a thought came to mind: puppies. So many puppies. My family on the floor rolling around with snuggly doodles. Yes, I felt I was wearing a helmet of needles like some psychotic horror movie, but those puppies. Thank God for those kids.

I counted down syringe by syringe and guess what? She didn't have enough to finish! They could not do more without further doctor approval and felt I had been through enough, so we called it a day.

No worries, I get to have at it again in four weeks.

I did ask what her typical injections are like and she replied eight to ten. Any guesses how many shots were injected for me today? Take a guess. Nineteen, twenty-eight, thirty-one? Survey says...forty! New Personal Best for the nurse! forty freaking shots. My body may have still been shaking from a mix of adrenaline and pain, but I was feeling pretty badass. My kids were proud. I was proud. We went out for Frosty's and all shared times were scared, brave and proud. We had a moment. I'm grateful for it.

Today's lessons:
- You have to be scared to be brave. You can't have one without the other.
- The very thing that you hate (like this disease) can also make you grateful.

Every day is a new opportunity. Hopefully your does not include needles.

Dark Clouds Creeping

Most days I'm accepting of myself. My faults. My imperfections. I believe in owning what God gave me with a positive attitude. Buuuuut... I really, like, really don't want to lose my hair.

I just don't.

As much as I'd love to embrace it, yell "Screw it!", I'm not there. I'd love to have a "Buy some wigs and have fun with it," attitude but I'm not feeling it. Please don't tell me to get one for every day of the week to show my personality! Mind you, they cost a black-market body part and are not known for comfort.

I'm a thirty-eight-year-old mom working on being secure in herself just like the rest of you. I don't want to lose my hair.

Don't want the three times a day head foam. I'll gladly take that thirty minutes of my life back. I, for sure, don't want the shots, which I've clearly explained. I know. I know - the struggle is part of the story. Blah, blah, blah. I have a notebook of all the sweet, little quotes to help you motivate and accept for yourself. But, to be honest, I just don't want to lose my damn hair. Is it strange to choose vanity over personality? Not totally, maybe just a smidge?

While I try to fill my head with calm, inspirational blurbs, what really fills my head are the following:
- People will stare.
- They will assume I have Cancer.
- My kids will be embarrassed by me.
- My husband will see me as "less than" beautiful.
- My kid's friends will tease them about their bald mom.
- It won't come back. Like, ever.

Now, before you freak out and start calling some help lines to report me- These are NOT my thoughts all of the time. I assure you that I am one happy girl. There are plenty of happy, grateful and what so many refer to as #blessed moments in my life. Plenty. However, nothing lasts forever. Everything is temporary, including the good moments. Even when you're enjoying a perfectly good day, get a good workout or have a great conversation with a loved one, the nagging struggle of real-life sets in. Much like you, I assume, deep cloudy thoughts can creep up your toes and slowly make their way to your head.

I am fortunate to have the tools to push them out, fight with them as I find the good again and again. This is life with chronic illness of ANY kind. This is why 60-80% of people JUST LIKE ME will face some sort of depression. For me, the clouds clear easily. I've worked really hard on my mental toolbox and have a variety of proven strategies. Thank God. It does not mean I am "owning my struggle" 100% of the time. It means I'm human. It means I'm scared. It means, I don't want to lose my hair.

For today, the sun is out. My kids have camp (Hallelujah! Hallelujah!) and we are having friends over for dinner. Life is good. Now, please excuse me while I go pick out my hat for the day.

Wigging Out

This, right here, is my noggin. My fuzzy, patchy, less than perfect melon. But, it's mine. This is me and it's time. Enough hiding out at in the safety of my home. I've decided I'm going to get a wig.

I'm doing the medical routine. I'm do the physical and emotional work. And I'm being patient with my body. The inside is beginning to heal, I can literally feel it in my gut. But here's the honest-to-goodness truth, I've lost 60-70% of my hair and although there is slight regrowth, nothing can come in as fast as it is coming out. Also, there is no guarantee the regrowth will stick around. Alopecia is an unpredictable beast without a guaranteed path. We just can't know what it will do next, if anything.

Being emotionally ready for a wig has been a hurdle, or more like a 52" box jump for you fitness enthusiasts. You look at it and say, "Oh, hell no! Ain't NO way I'm ready for that. Ain't NO way!" It's too much of a commitment to the disease because it's accepting it completely. It means accepting that I may never have hair again, a terrifying pill to swallow. And, yet, here I am looking at that box and thinking, "You know what? I think I can handle that."

So, what's taken me so long to get here?
- I was really optimistic I would not lose all of my hair. (Some AA folks only lose patches and nothing more.)
- I was sure things would grow back faster. (Silly me and my optimistic ways.)
- I thought headbands and hats would NOT get old. (So damn old.)
- Um...denial. Duh!

What's shifted? (Remember "Shift, Sip and Simmer".)
- I've had enough hat wearing for a lifetime.
- Headbands, even the wide ones, don't cover the damage.
- I would like to go out to dinner without thinking about which eating establishments find hats acceptable.
- I want to go on dates and feel "girly". (Insert eye roll.)
- I've been putting off church lately considering the difficulty of coverage there.
- I'm incredibly bored of solid tops that accent my patterned headbands. I'm just a girl who wants to wear a damn patterned shirt!
- I want to look like me again. Sigh...

Wigs are incredibly expensive, itchy and uncomfortable, although they have come a LONG way. But I do feel like I'm hiding a little bit and I don't like that feeling. Hiding makes me feel weak and lonely and I'm not in to those feelings. However, I'm not 100% owning my patchy head in public just yet either.

I hope to get there. Until then, I want to feel some sense normal. Some sense of me.

A girlfriend of mine had recommended me to a local, well known salon that specializes in hair loss. We got coverage for our kids tomorrow while we head in for a consult to see what my options are. I'm actually really excited, now that I'm open to this, about hanging with my fellow hair deprived friends and finding a look that works for me. I'm giving Alopecia a slight nod, as if to show it my acceptance. It's an opportunity to move forward and stop sitting in the unknown. I'm choosing the next path, not alopecia. So, I guess you could say, I'm bringing Angie back.

Savannah Oh Na Na

Oh. My. Word.

Take a seat, my dears. Hold a hand because life is UNBELIEVABLY topsy turvy. Have a seat, I've got a story for you.

I've been trying to process the last 24 hours of the most bizarre, uplifting, uncomfortable, yet euphoric experience. I can't believe people do this every day. I mean, talk about wanting to laugh and cry at the same time. That's the best way to wrap it up.

Wig Fitting Day!

Headed to my appointment, I put on a sundress, make-up, a ball cap and heals. Because if you can't feel fancy at wig fitting, is life even worth living? Obviously, I had to stop for gas considering it had been on E for a minimum of 3 days, which is how I continue to live life on the edge. How skinny can I make that little red line? Anyway, I hopped out to fill up and realized how I must have looked wearing a bargain Old Navy dress, inappropriately high wedges and a ratty old' ball cap. Then it popped in my head, like breaking open a bottle of champagne. Holy Moly- I am TOTALLY trying to find balance wearing a ball cap and heals! That is my life's journey! Brain explosion mid gas pump because aren't we all a little ball cap and a little bit high heel?

For the first time, I walked into Jeffrey Paul's Hair & Scalp Specialists in Cleveland, Ohio BALD HEADED! Yes, little shy, often awkward, me! And I did not die. I thought I might when I stepped out of the car and walked through the parking lot. I would not have been surprised if I died while waiting to talk to the receptionist. But I didn't. It was weird. So weird, but life went on as I waited impatiently wearing red lips and no hair. Hell, yeah, we can do hard things.

I can NOT say enough about the Jeffery Paul Salon. It's just not possible. I will say that it is a salon of passion, big hearts and experts. They know what the heck they are doing and THRIVE on making people feel good. The fitting began with a WHOLE lot of hair- knowing that they can make it less and cannot make it more.

You guys, my friends, I can honestly say that the moment I put it on there was no "Oh my goodness. I love it," moment. In fact, I wanted to run out screaming. It felt too much. It looked too foreign. It was overwhelmingly unrecognizable. I could not see myself in there and it was heartbreaking. I doubted the whole, need a second mortgage, experience.

But because I'm a pleaser and didn't want to hurt anyone's feelings. I said nothing. I took a breath. I willed myself to be patient and push through. And laughed a little when I figured I won't look any worse. After a bit of deep breathing, I asked lots of questions and, although it was so damn hard- I was honest. And my stylist was a gift from the heavens. Like, wrapped in a cloth of angels and carried down to earth just for me. She sensed my discomfort and reassured me throughout the two-hour consult. We thinned it out. We trimmed it up. We talked and talked. Snip by snip, I began to see myself again. I, oh, so slowly, recognized my eyes, saw the strength of where I'd been and just kept breathing. Be still and know.

I began to feel okay, again. I looked down at my wrists, covered in bracelets and rings given to me by my incredible friends and family. Things like *Strength*, *You've got this, we've got you*, and *Nothing can dim the light that shines within*. My favorite ring from my husband representing easier days. A bracelet from a girl's trip to remind me of their support. My heavens, how can you not move forward when those are the things hugging your wrists and fingers?

The hair was just so perfect. And I've had crappy hair for most of my life, minus when I was pregnant. I was a mix between a news broadcaster and a southern politician's wife- feeling very much like a Savannah. Bless your heart. Oh, my word. I might start talking in a southern accent. The realization that I could do this was intense, y'all. I was going to be okay after all.

After a thirty-minute tutorial on how to care for her (Savannah), I was on my way. As my phone was BOOMING with support from my people, I sat in my luxurious minivan and cried. For what, I'm not totally sure. Just a release. More letting go (which I discovered is NEVER ending). More finding who I'm meant to be. Life is a holy emotional roller coaster. And I cannot change that. But I CAN savor the top of that coaster and I sure as hell can survive the bottom.

My word, it has been a journey. But one I am grateful for. As weird and soul searching as it has been. It is my journey and I'm going to hair-flip my way through it. A little ball cap and a little high heel. I'm a lucky girl and there's no way around it.

I'm Just Not Precious

Oh, my goodness YES. YES. And YES. So much freaking YES! If you are precious, first of all- God Bless you. I love precious people. I honestly do.

I love that they love volunteering and baking for people. I love that they love everything about motherhood (because some people really do!) and don't really drink and swear much. You go and be your precious self! Be proud of your preciousness!

I have tried to be precious, too. I've tried pretending that everything about motherhood is a blessing and that the moment I held my baby for the first time was fulfilling a new level of magic I never knew existed. It wasn't though. I didn't know what to think when they put that baby in my arms except that I was tired and in pain. I was not overwhelmed with love that first moment. I wasn't even sure my baby was that cute!

(Let's pause here and hold back judgement, please. OF COURSE, I love my children. I would walk to the ends of the world for them. But some moms feel it that first moment, and I did not. I do now- but it was more fear than magic at first.) See? Not so precious.

I say bad words. I often forget to call people back. I don't eat organic and clean as much as I should. I could volunteer more. I probably use too many sandwich baggies and chemicals when I clean. I am a not-so-precious work in progress.

More non-precious thoughts:

- I am the only human who sheds more on the dog (hypoallergenic) than the dog does on the human.

- I found one of my hairs in my homemade risotto the other night. I cried with laughter realizing "I only have about 76 hairs, and now one of them is in my risotto!" What sort of twisted universe is this?

- I still wrap my head in my towel after I shower. It falls off every SINGLE time because I do not have enough hair to hold it up. But I keep doing it. Creature of habit, I guess.

- With each shower, I squirt the same amount of shampoo and conditioner in my hand as always. This is NOT precious for two reasons. 1) Half of it runs down my face burning my eyes and mouth. Gross. Don't drink your shampoo, friends. 2) Between the bald spots and baby hairs coming in- there is just NO need for that much hair product. I could be saving some money here.

I could be more precious in how I deal with these situations, but honestly, it's just so funny to me. I used to want to be precious, for people to say "Oh, Angie? I know, isn't she just so precious?" I've decided to let precious people be precious, and for me to just be me.

(Side note- If you're into podcasts, Jen Hatmaker's "For the Love" is a great one, whether you're precious or not. But, especially if you're not.)

Things Are Happening

The world can be such a supportive force. Once you put it out there, your people will come calling. About six months after my hair started falling out, the original bald spots began filling in. Those are actually some pretty incredible results. Not a day goes by that I don't realize that. At first it looks like subtle, dark shadows. Some people experience itching or tingling as it grows in, or even tenderness. I felt that way when I was losing hair. Meaning, I could tell what was falling out next due to the itching and tenderness. There were no physical symptoms of regrowth for me. Through my social media support groups, it sounds like every story is completely different. There just isn't a rhyme or reason to any of it.

Once it started growing, it was a fast-moving machine. Coming in thicker and curlier than I'd seen it since my early twenty's. Likely my hair had, in recent years, been thin and brittle due to the long-term effects of my prednisone and other heavy medications. The new color was a mix of salt and pepper, which was not at all surprising knowing that I had been going grey since my early thirty's. And to be honest, it could come in purple and I would have been just as happy. As you can see in pictures, I still had two spots of original hair. There was a wisp of bangs in the front and a thin, straggly piney tail in the back. This was surprisingly convenient because I could continue pulling off a hat, or large bohemian style bandana. If you were to run your fingers through it, you would find twenty-five to thirty-five Skittle sized bald spots. However, at the time I wrote this, they were covered with teeny, tiny scabs from the previous day's injections making my head look like a combination of a topographic map and a battle field.

That's another ridiculous thing about Alopecia Areata, some people lose every hair on their pretty little heads while others only ever have golf ball size spots. Some people experience regrowth, and some will go their whole life without it. You get what you get. At this point, there is more unknown than known about this disease. Much like any autoimmune diseases you usually have more questions than there are answers. Considering 80% of my head was baby bald, I was truly appreciative of every sprout. Another funny thing is that you learn to be grateful, yet not get too excited. Anyone who is fortunate enough to experience regrowth also knows there is an equal possibility of losing it all again. So, you take what you can. One day at a time. You do your damndest not to look back and overthink it. Doctors do believe it's linked to stress, so you can't stress about it or it might fall out anyway. Accept it and move forward.

My current treatment for the last 5 months has been oral Xeljanz (used to treat RA), steroid injections to the scalp, prescription head foam and prescription shampoo. In terms of my self-care treatment, I am meditating, journaling, reading, hitting the gym five days a week and enjoying long walks with the dog. I have also found podcasts and proper nutrition play a large role. My mindset is my biggest advantage over this disease. Because with or without my hair, I am healing from the inside out. With or without my hair, I am going to live a kick ass life. With or without my hair, I am going to be okay. And that, my friends, is the beginning of everything.

Fingers crossed for a mullet for Halloween and a pixie cut for Christmas!

Don't Break My Heart

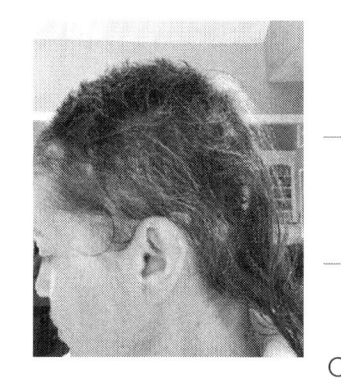

"Don't break my heart, my achy breaky heart," Billy Rae Cyrus.

So, who wore it better? Me, or early 90s Billy Rae Cyrus? It's a tough call. What's funny about it (and there is so much that is funny) is that he made a CHOICE. I did not. He chose to rock his mullet for a few too many years. However, this is not my idea of a sweet style for a lady in her late thirties.

Nothing about my condition or Alopecia has been my choice. NOTHING. More than that, nothing about this has been easy. NOTHING. My marriage, my kids, my life is forever changed by my hair loss. Please don't think I don't take this lightly. Yes, I use humor and sarcasm to cope with the crap. But I have lost plenty of sleep, cried plenty of tears and questioned plenty of relationships because of Alopecia Areata.

It sucks.
Every time I go to get dressed, it sucks.
Every time I shower, it sucks.
Every time I go to the gym overheating in my sporty ballcap, it sucks.

(Side note- "Sweat Proof" hats are a lie if you sweat like a five-hundred pound man running a marathon in the Sahara. Also, do you know sweat can literally drip in your ear canal? It's true for those us who don't have the hair to absorb it. Interesting fact, huh?)

It's been a challenge to feel beautiful in a scarf, ballcap, or even wearing my fancy wig, Savannah. A hell of a journey. I share a lot, as you know. But I don't always share the intense heartache of it. It could break your heart, your achy breaky heart. I just don't think you'd understand.

Here's what I know: The Alopecia was not my choice. The way I deal with it is 100% my choice. 100%. That's all the percent's, guys. All. Of. Them. Make a choice, not an excuse. It's either 100% your choice or 100% your excuse. I will NOT be defined by my excuses. I will happily be defined by my choices.

Every single day I get out of my bed and choose to be happy. Some days I have to fake it for those first few minutes. Happiness can be a challenge- there's a thousand excuses to be grumpy. Some days when the kids are fighting and spilling orange juice, and my hands aren't working yet, I have to dig DEEP to see the good. Usually it's little things that pick me back up: coffee, a DVR'd show, the dinner I have planned, or the funny thoughts in my head. You have to find your little slice of happy and focus on that until it's all you feel. Gratitude will save your life.

It is so much easier to yell and scream, or to feel sorry for yourself. So much simpler to lie in bed crying or watching Netflix. You know what makes me feel worse? Doing THAT! That exact scenario makes me feel sadder, weaker and more hopeless than ever.

I'm a big believer in the phrase "fake it 'til you make it." Parenting, positivity, confidence- life! If you do it long enough, it actually starts blooming in you. The gratitude becomes authentic because you realize it's not that hard to be happy. There is so much good out there, you just have to start small some days.

I had no idea Billy Rae would inspire this writing due to his CHOICE of hairstyle. But now he's got me reflecting on many levels, much like his hair. Here's hoping you found your happy today and that I'll be rocking a pixie cut by Christmas.

Billy Rae just might be my spirit animal, or a kick ass Halloween costume. What am I grateful for today? I was bald on the 4th, I've got Billy Rae by Halloween and dreaming of a pixie by Christmas. We've all got goals, but that's pretty hard to top.

Preach

I used a hair dryer this morning.
It's fine that it only took seven minutes.
In fact, it's fabulous.
God is good.
Amen.

Holy Haircut

So, I'm kind of freaking our because I just pulled into a hair salon in my little town because I have a hair appointment. Now, before you all think I've lost my damn mind, I did not make this appointment. My husband, bless his soul, actually made me a haircut and color without my permission. Apparently, he has grown tired of my sweet mullet or has at least grown tired of me complaining about it. I'm not sure. Either way, he knew that I would never call to make the appointment. He knew I'd be awkward trying to explain all my random straggles and various lengths of hair. He knew I was terrified. Because calling and making that appointment would mean letting go of all of my original hair.

And he was absolutely right.

Yet another example of why we need to let people in. We need to be honest. We need to lean on people in times of struggle. Now before I start sounding like a country song and get out my guitar, I'm a firm believer in being independent. I am totally on board with people handling their own mess. But sometimes, it's too heavy. It's just too much and you need a little nudge. A slight push. That's what he did and that's what I needed. Growing up a comfort zone kind of girl, I would have stayed hidden in my ball cap and Savannah without that nudge. It was time to let it go. Literally.

So, he called. Booked it. He did his best to tell them what I needed which included a hair color situation. Something totally new to him and quite comical to overhear. I'm just going to go with it, I guess. And if I can live with a bald or spotty head for a few months and figure out a way to be comfortable with that, then I think I can find a way to be comfortable with a pixie or buzz cut. Whatever they decide to do can't be worse than what I've been through, right?

I am ready to get rid of my salt and pepper up top. And my gut tells me it's time to move forward rather than sitting in this uncomfortable in-between land. It's easy to be comfortable here, yet I'm not totally myself either. I figure it's time to rely on some cute, big earrings, bold lipstick and mascara. Dress it up. Have a little fun with it and let it go.

I may be sweating in my puffy vest. My hands are shaking like leaves as I write this, but I know this is just another bump in the road. I have done harder things than this and survived so just put one foot in front of the other.

Snip. Snip. Off I go.

R.I.P Mullet

Sitting in that chair was as uncomfortable as it was powerful. It was one of those cute, little boutique salons where everyone is in the open and there is no little wall to protect you. I sat with my hat on for as long as I could trying not to notice the posh, sophisticated people on either side of me. Close enough to hold hands, or maybe pat my bald head. My husband had called ahead and told the salon about my situation and let them know I was anxious; however, I do not believe that the message had been passed on to my stylist. Or maybe they had, and she was simply trying to be polite and not pry. She was very sweet and a gentle listener but seemed as nervous and timid as I was.

Taking my hat off was like that feeling when you have a dream that your naked walking down a school hallway or something. It's a heavy weight of embarrassment and almost happens in slow motion. You know when you feel the heat in your face almost like you are watching yourself in third person? That's how I would describe the moment I took off my hat. To be honest, I don't know if anyone was watching me at that moment. I as too scared to look. I just stared straight into the mirror, into my own familiar eyes and took a breath. This was one of those moments you can't turn back from. Moving forward was the only option.

All of a sudden, I had an urge to just get it over with. Go on with the show. From that look on, the stylist was more nervous than I was. I could tell she was trying to keep my original hairs. For example, my bangs had not fallen out, so she used those to my advantage and incorporated them into the pixie. My favorite moment was the final snip of the straggly, mullet hair in the back. After feeling the air on my neck, I literally stopped so that I could take a picture of it for documentation. I wanted to remember that moment.

Exhale.
Release.
Leave it all on the floor.

192

We added a cute, dark brown color with a hint of red. Added a little product to make it "piecey" followed by a brief style session. I waltzed out of there like Mary Tyler Moore in her television introduction years ago. I was ready to throw my hat in the hair and yell "you're going to make it after all." Because, I was. I was going to make it after all. I took my positive 1970s vibes down to the local carry-out sandwich shop and ordered a fancy salad to-go after stopping to take a selfie in the bathroom.

Until this point, I did not realize how the things you fear the most can be the same things that build you up. I had a new sense of courage, power and pride to go with my new cut. And looking back now, I can say it was only the beginning.

Put in the Work

Put in the work.
Have a little faith.
And you will see progress.

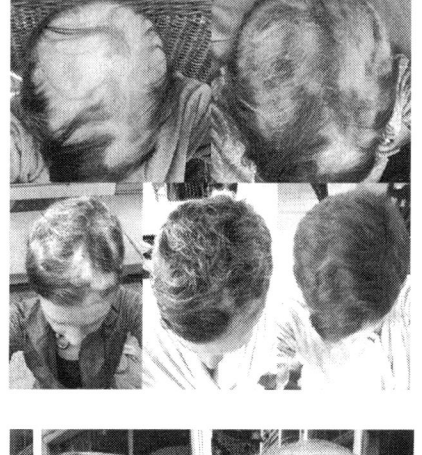

These are pictures of a four-month span of treatment. It was a consistent use of steroid injections, topical foam, prescription shampoo and Xeljanz. It was work. As I've emphasized before, I put equal focus, if not more on my self-care treatment including meditation, journaling, fitness and nutrition. In every way, I have put in the work. Each morning, each afternoon and every night. I physically and mentally put in the work.

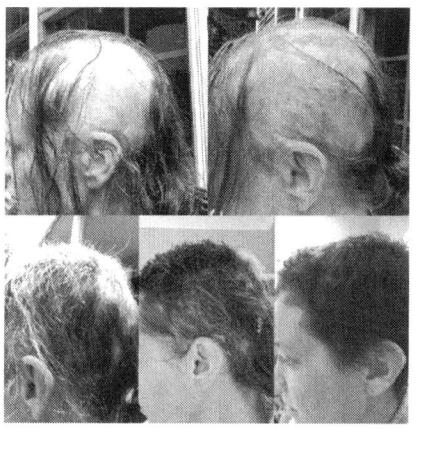

Some days were easier than others. As with any struggle, there are days where it's a little easier to see the bright side, to feel the support and to have a little faith. You know those days when the coffee it just right or the kids seem to get along. When you get a random call from an old friend or a surprise in the mail, you're able to hold on to your faith a little more gently. You know those are good days, because you've also had the days when you had to hold on to your faith, your piece of mind with a clenched fist.

Yes, some days were easier, but every day was hard. Days are still hard, now I'm just better prepared to handle them. The adjustment in my thinking, the shifting of it would be the hardest part of my journey. The medical side was easy! Take the pills, use the foam, eat the kale. Fine, whatever. Those choices might take discipline, but they do not make you dig deep into your insecurities. They don't make you question how your body deals with its emotions, both good and bad. What you have control over (which is so much more than you think) and what you don't. How you have gotten to this place and where you can go from here.

The "work" I'm referring to is asking and answering the question- ok, so now what? I've got this situation. One that I did not choose, yet here I am. Where do I go from here? What do I want my life to look like? What is my body trying to tell me? There is no easy answer and no magic pill. It's you verse you and holy moly does it take work. For me it's taken a lot of writing, praying, crying, questioning and reading from people who inspire me. Which has led to quieting the mind, deep breathing and reaching out to people. In return, I was given deeper connections to the people who matter most, a stronger faith and an opportunity to share my story. The biggest gift from my work and my faith is an intensely overwhelming confidence in myself and awareness of what I want my life to look like.

I mean, how many people can honestly say that? I love who I'm becoming and it's because of this experience that I get to feel this way. I was telling my husband the other day how I love the way I look at life now and it's because I lost my hair. He laughed as I went on to say that it would have been nice to have this shift in thinking without going bald. But maybe it's a lesson I needed. Maybe I wasn't listening to myself before. Either way, it's done and I'm better off for it. Guess what, though? You don't! You can change your life or health or way of thinking as you are right now, without finding your hair in the shower drain. If you are reading this right now and feeling inspired. I'm telling ya, you have an opportunity. So, what are you going to do with it?

How Quickly We Forget

As I was driving to pick up my kids yesterday, I was annoyed at how my hair was tickling my neck. Let's just rewind that thought. I was actually annoyed at the way my hair was tickling my neck. Then I literally said out loud to myself, "Man, my hair is getting really long!"

I immediately caught the humor in my conversation with myself and nearly pulled off the road in laughter.

1. I was talking to myself
2. My hair length was annoying me
3. I acted as if my three-inch-long hairs were competing with Rapunzel. Like they were just SOOO long.

How quickly we forget what we've been praying and working for, right?

Life is funny and I have a hair appointment tomorrow.

Chapter Eight: Friendships Can Save Your Life

My Chosen People

I'm taking a minute to celebrate the fact that I just have so many people and am so very lucky. This is something I have always known. My family, I mean, the words do not exist to give justice to the love of my family. But I cannot tell my story without giving props to my friends. The amazing, beautiful, imperfect people I chose to be in my life. Even better than that, they chose ME to be in their lives.

After moving to California as a thirty-six-year-old mother of two, I was open and ready to meet more of *my people*. Well here I am, nine months later, and still no people. I have found many nice people, with sweet smiles and kind waves of "hello." But, when I start to share myself with comments like "Oh, man I was so frustrated with my son I was ready to leave him on the curb," I hear crickets. Hmm? Come on! So, we aren't those kinds of friends, then? We aren't going to share our imperfections here on the playground. Oh, okay! Let me smack that smile back on and tell you how fulfilled I am as stay-home mom and wife. Oh, it's just a gift and I am the luckiest!

That's kind of bullshit, right? I am not crazy to admit that parenting, being a wife and woman with a passion is NOT easy. Why do we have to make it look seamless when seams put things together? You cannot create things without the seams. Can we just stop pretending that life is filled with seamless stories? Come on, people! Let's make mistakes, be honest about them and lift each other up.

This morning, I spent over two hours on the phone with a friend I met in seventh grade. That's right, seventh grade. And she is not the only childhood friend I am close to. How many people are able to do that? When I moved out to Cali, I assumed other ladies had a group of middle and high school friends that they kept in touch with. Wow, not so much. Don't get me wrong, we don't talk as frequently as we used to and see each other even less. This one, in particular is in Pittsburg although the majority are in Columbus, Ohio (this is MY town, too). These are the type of people that a million miles and years could come between you, and it would mean nothing. Nada. We pick up right where we left off.

Here's the thing with my chosen people, we know each other's imperfections. We may fight about them, laugh about them and mainly, accept each other for them. Anyone of us can tell you who will be early, late or even forget to show up to a monthly dinner. And guess what, we don't care. If I tell them that I currently have two kids for sale on Craigslist, they will respond with "Cool, how much are you asking for them?" and then encourage me to go pour myself a glass of wine. That's the kind of love we give out. No crickets in this circle. No judgment here, folks.

And the laughing. I mean, you guys. The laughing is insane. We have annoyed our fair share of bartenders, cab drivers and even lovely people seated at the table next to us. There is just such ease to our happiness. These are the people that know all of my stories and secrets and guard them safely in their back pockets. They hold them there for me when I need to be reminded of them and if I am having a hard time remembering them for myself. Close to twenty years of memories that cannot be erased, even if some of them should be. (That's a whole other chapter.) I only hope I have been the same friend in return. One of the ladies will quickly tell you that one of my imperfections is my horrible memory. She can recall every detail, where I am at a loss for the day of the week.

Another weakness of mine is not always making them aware of my pain. Because, like with my family, I want them to think that I am strong and can do it all. Here's the thing, though, I know without a doubt they will climb a mountain for me. If I need it, whatever "it" may be, they are there. They will be organizing, plotting, praying and delegating on my behalf should I say the word. I am right there, in their back pocket. They are keeping me safe and loved, without even knowing it.

It took me a two-hour conversation, across the country, to remember the gift that my chosen people are in my life. Yes, we had to plan the conversation around school drop-off and naps, but we did it. And now, I am sitting a little higher because I am holding their secrets and stories in my back pocket.

Girlfriends Make You Feel Alive

My days are good. My days are happy and fulfilling. There really isn't much I would change about my life. I walk around content with who I am. But sometimes it takes a break from the grind to remember who I am outside of the home.

Enter - Girls night.

A hysterical, chaotic, stumbling reminder that I am still a little bit wild, immature, and a hell of a good time! There are no rules, no cutting food and no filters. I've never had a great filter anyway, so this is a relief. We say what we want and throw caution to the wind! Walking the streets without worrying about little people crossing safety and our only agenda includes a small nap and dinner reservations.

Friends have an incredible ability to remind you that you are relevant, beautiful and downright awesome. And I get to be that person for them. You can laugh at each other's imperfections without taking anything personal. Because you know they love you and no one is keeping score. I feel updated on new handbags and the latest trends in skincare. Although, these are not things high on my priority list (as my friends know), we can laugh about it. Let's be honest, it sure as hell beats helping my family look for their shoes on a Saturday night.

They know your secrets, your struggles and are willing to talk it through or leave it be if it gets to be too much. You feel safe, supported and most of all- like you.

I appreciate that we have our differences. I complain about a BS call at the Cav's game, and they spend the first 10 min scoping out Khloe Kardashian. They subtly tote their adorable little classy, clutches, while I carry on about my new navy wristlet I got from Marshalls. (Which I almost didn't purchase because I didn't want to fork over the $16.00 it cost me.)

Regardless of these differences, they are also the first to ask me the hard questions, first in line to reassure me- about parenting, about health, all of it. They remind me to treat myself to life's little luxuries. They encourage me to take care of myself. They use my own Grandmom's term "snip-nose" with the same love and affection as me when making it a part of their vocabulary.

We talk about hard things. Emotional, weepy, heavy topics. Real life pain and struggles are now part of our life. Gone are the days of little problems. We've hit the ugly side of adulthood. It gets heated when all that love and passion is jumbled together. But it ends with tears of laughter and a slightly sarcastic joke. Every. Single. Time. We leave hand-in-hand asking strangers to take our picture in the street. Leave no man behind.

This is what girlfriends do. They send obnoxious memes. Plan trips. And follow through the next day with texts like "Are you alive?" In return, there are messages of "Where are you? Are you kidnapped?", even when we are at the same bar. You can never be too careful! We have to keep our friends safe in this scary world!

It's easy to forget how much we matter in the world, and that we need each other. I didn't realize I needed that reminder until after the fact. It feels pretty damn good to be accepted for all of my ridiculousness, and for me to do that for them. Whether your army is big or small, they need you as much as you need them. Get out and get away. It feels good to be reminded that life exists outside of my front door and so do I.

Lessons from "We Time"

Pretty sure my girlfriends and I solved all the problems, shared all the feelings and drank all the drinks. Mission accomplished. Boom. In a matter of forty-eight hours away from any responsibility, we managed to remind ourselves of some very important truths.

Here's what we learned.

1. "It's fine" is the biggest lie there ever was in the world. "Fine" is a BS excuse, don't buy it. Dig deeper.
2. Choose. Make a choice. Make a change. Who the hell cares? It's your life. Own the role of "you." The one's who matter will encourage it.
3. You have more power, more support, more in common with others than you know. Choose to see it and share it. You may even find it with someone unexpected.
4. The more you speak your truth, the more your people come to you. So, shout that shit from the mountaintops.
5. People come into your life for a reason. Yes, there is a greater plan. But also, yes? You make the choice to see them. Don't let that opportunity pass you by because you're insecure.
6. People WILL have your back. Just TELL them you need it. Speak up!
7. They say you have to be a friend to make a friend. Turns out, you just have to be you, be real and show up.
8. Belly giggles that turn into tears are alive and well! Age does not change this.
9. Swimming in the rain at thirty-eight is just as exhilarating as it was at 8.
10. Take the trip. ALWAYS take the trip.

Girlfriends are a gift. They can save your life and will likely save the world.

All the Yeses!

Have you ever tried to jump on an inflatable device in a pool? You know the kind. It can be a raft, swan, or any blow-up tube. It's not easy due to it bouncing around in the water and you wearing a bathing suit. Recently I went on a girl trip and there was an inflatable bull in the pool. Obviously, we were going to give that thing a try but what we didn't know is what it would teach us.

Life is like riding an inflatable bull, in the rain, after too much champagne. I mean, that's a hell of a metaphor. But I can't think of anything more accurate at this phase of my life.

Exhilarating.
Frustrating.
Hysterical.
Disappointing- All the yeses.
You fail and fall. Again, and again.

You find your focus. And just when you think you've got it? BAM. There you are with one foot in the water and the other tangled in plastic like a pretzel. You're left thinking, *How the hell did I get here? I had a plan! I should have been able to handle that! I thought I was strong enough to hold on!*

Do you see where I'm going here? It didn't matter how intricate my master plan was to stay on that bull. Some things are simply out of your control. That weekend we assigned the bull the name Ferdinand Alpha. Being inspired by the "Bring It On" look in his eyes we quickly realized he had different plans, just like life. And it turns out my planning and preparation didn't matter at all. Yes, I figured out how to gracefully climb aboard. Yes, with some practice I was able to hold on longer (lots of inner thigh squeezing and core strength). Yes, I was enjoying that cowboy hat more than necessary.

Even with all of that positivity- I fell every damn time. Every single attempt left me gasping for air, half drowning in the water. Before this metaphor spins into a downward spiral of darkness and disparity - here's the GOOD stuff. (And I'm so in love with the good stuff.)

1.*Falling off/falling down, can actually be pretty hysterical. Like, a belly giggle that starts in your toes making it hard to breath situation. Go ahead and LAUGH at it when fitting, because it feels amazing.*

2. *Get back UP. Try again. Do the things. Brush it off and grab it by the horns! (Pun intended.)*

3. *When you fall, and you will fall repeatedly, look around. Who's there? This is my most favorite part! People will pick you up. Literally UNTANGLE you from the mess that is your life. They will check on you. They are the first to give you a new strategy for the next time. SEE those people. Appreciate them. Let them push you. Let them pull you. And by all means, let them help you.*

Life is not YOU vs. Ferdinand Alpha Bull.
Life is US vs. Ferdinand Alpha Bull.

Embrace the Victory and the Defeat

"Vulnerability is not knowing victory or defeat; it's understanding the necessity of both; it's engaging. It's being all in." Brené Brown (Daring Greatly)

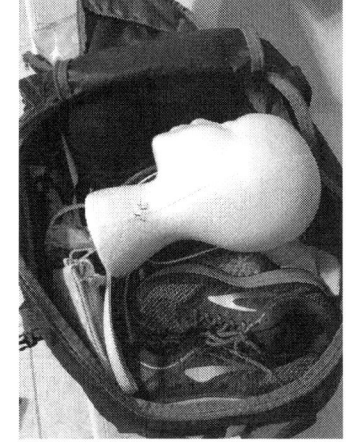

Seriously, guys. If this picture isn't the perfect example of that, I don't know what is. Pretty sure this image would be found in the dictionary under "Examples of Vulnerability." How many of you have packed a manikin head to support your wig, because what's the point of having a crumpled-up wig, and a pair of heels?

Can we just talk about victory and defeat for a quick sec? Glennon Doyle Melton would refer to this as 'Brutiful,' the combination of beauty and brutal. Life HAS to have both. There is no freaking way around it. You can NOT have one without the other and still be REAL. A life someone claims to be all victory or all beauty? You guys, it's lies. Fakity fake fake, and I cannot do it. Cannot handle that. So many men and women I meet these days are sick, tired and drained from all the fakeness. People crave authenticity. I promise, they do.

It's taken a lifetime of experience. Yes, all thirty-eight years of it. Sometimes in the trenches, and other days in the beauty of the clouds. I've needed to live through both. See it for myself and feel the balance of the two. I feel like these are truths we all know, yet still don't talk about it. We don't give ourselves permission to admit that we have so much fear, anger and sadness while simultaneously being happy. When I do say it out loud to people, I can see them exhale. As if to say, "Yes. Thank you. That's how I feel, too." Here is your permission slip to be vulnerable and honest.

This is my suitcase from my weekend trip with some remarkable women who are such supporters of vulnerability as a strength. It's probably the funniest picture I've taken in years. I mean, it's hysterical and boarder-line disturbing, right? My bag has adorable wedges, and a freaking mannequin head. A damn foam head!

I can hardly write it without cracking up on the airplane sitting next to an adorable four-year-old who is losing his mind. This is for real, right? It's actually happening to me, not a character in a sitcom. I really had to pack a mannequin head in my suitcase? (Mind you, I opted for "checked" luggage, so I did not have to be there when it went through security. I do have a limit on who all needs to see my vulnerability.)

So, this foam head of mine, it could have been a symbol of defeat. A sign of struggle. Weakness. Imperfection in this society. Inadequacy to many. Less than perfect. And, it's definitely NOT precious. (She literally has pins in her eyes because my kids think it's funny.) Some women, and even men, would get depressed by it or maybe stay hidden in the safety of their homes. Many people would not be willing to risk vulnerability by taking a trip.

But you know what's incredible about the defeat of the foam head? It's surrounded by victory. Literally surrounded by signs of strength and progress. (First the pain, then the rising!) I did mention I was headed to the sunshine state, right? Kid free. Great group of girls. No kids. (I wrote that twice for a reason.) What in the WORLD is more victorious than that?

Bring on that damn defeat. Bring it every day that it leads to victory. I'll take that creepy foam head as long as it comes with wedges and long weekends. Although, I'd give my last eighty-seven hairs to see the TSA worker's reaction as my bag moved through the scanner! Do you think they did a second look to make sure it was a fake head? Can you imagine the ridiculous things they see each day?

How's that for vulnerability? Embrace the victory and the defeat, you guys. Because it's SO much better than the alternative.

Oh, the SHAME! Ladies, Ladies, Ladies

We are the biggest cheerleaders for our children and spouses, so why is it that we are NOT that for each other? I've had more than a few moms confide in me the pressures of motherhood. Although the whole idea of "Mom-shaming" from society and social media may seem to be trending, let me assure you- these feelings are FOR REAL! It's not just a trend. The demands and expectations have never been higher, and we need to talk about it.

You all read my truth and struggles to live up to a certain Pinterest level of parenting and "wifing". So, I decided to investigate more versions of truths. I interviewed a few of my mom friends from young, first time moms, experienced moms, divorced moms, married ones, working and stay home, and everything in-between mom's.

I also felt it was necessary to gather actual research from some respected professionals. This is the real deal, you guys. The facts, stories and heart from the many angles of mothering.

Facts:
- 75% of women are NOT satisfied with their friendships.
- Friendships are crucial to physical health as proven my MRI brain scans.
- Loneliness is the #1 health issue of our time (New York Times)
- It is as damaging as smoking 15 cigarettes a day if you don't feel supported in your life.
- Not feeling supported is the equivalent to the physical damage of a lifelong alcoholic.
**How loved and supported you feel is the largest predictor of your health 20 years down the road. **(Shasta Nelson, "Frientimacy")

Major light bulb moment for me while researching the health effects of friendships when I realized EVERY specialist, I have seen for my physical health has asked more questions about my support systems than my physical symptoms. Isn't that interesting?

After talking with moms living varying lifestyles, here are their actual experiences. These are the things we worry about:

- *"The stigma with medicating our kids is intense (on both ends). Never in a million years when I was pregnant did I think this would be my child's reality. It is not the "easy way out." It is a full-time, daily job to manage what is best for him." She is well aware of the looks suggesting "Geez, can't she just discipline them or teach them how to listen?" Well aware of the stares. If any of you have had to go through the medication dilemma, then you can feel this mama's pain.*

- *For you working moms, trying to find the balance is tough. And many women are better moms BECAUSE they work! One mom describes it as, "Yes, I'm tired from staying up late and making a cute back-to-school signs because if my kid asks me one more time to pick him up, I'll BURST!" This mom is lucky to have a flexible job that allows her to volunteer from time to time and be the Surprise Reader. Even then, "those eye rolls that I just don't need add to the already craziness that is life." When is it ever enough? You work too much- eye roll. You work too little- eye roll.*

- *And don't get me started on the food debate! Apparently other mom's feel the heat to provide 100% organic, raw fruit and veggie filled lunches as well. "We have all felt the judgement for not using enough organic foods or volunteering enough."*

The number one confession the moms I interviewed shared was that they are all former mom-judgers. Meaning, they may have judged or assumed things about parenting BEFORE they were parents themselves. They were also very quick to explain how they have shifted and become more empathetic in general. Experience has opened their eyes and allowed empathy and imperfection to take over.

- *As one mom describes it, "I've learned to have more empathy and see things from different perspectives. We all parent differently and that's okay!"*

- *"Nobody is perfect and in the days of social media I think we forget that because pictures and captions can glorify even the smallest moments."*
- *"Experience- the older my kids get, the more I have opened my eyes".*
- *"As a younger mom, I worried too much about the perfect image. Now, I admire moms who take time for themselves and that is what inspires me."*

It's not you, it's me…Overwhelmingly, I've discovered that we put more pressure on ourselves than we do on each other. The moms I talked to aren't that concerned about YOU because they are so concerned about living up to their own standard of "good enough!"

- *"I am my own worst judge. I'm not actually concerned about other moms! I sweat the small stuff too much for me and mine- not for other moms."*
- *"No, I don't know how the preschool line works because I've never done it!"*
- *"In a world of crazy talented, brilliant kids, what if mine is average? Am I building up their confidence to feel 'good enough' in such a competitive society?"*
-

Here's what I know for sure: 1. We admit to being mom-shamers/judgers BEFORE we were moms, but we know better now. 2. We are our own WORST judges. 3. Most importantly, we need each other. Actually, according to Jen Hatmaker, "We are wired to need each other."

So, what can we do about it?
- *"Give each other a break. Our best is still enough!"*
- *"It's all about balance. But, you know, it's okay to be the one to sign-up for napkins!"* (In reality, napkins are probably the most important item at a school party.)
- *"I'm grateful for 'all hands-on deck'! It really takes a village and we need to help each other."*
- *"If everyone was just a little nicer, smiled a little more…it would go a long way."*

Biggest response: Choose people who support you!
- *"I try to find friends with similar viewpoints and parenting styles."*

-   *"Quality over quantity. Surround yourself with a few people who honestly make you feel heard and supported. Find a network of mom's who "get" you."* (Mom groups, church, gym, etc.)

Favorite suggestion- *"PRIORITIES! Let's give high-fives's for kids that are alive, fed and occasionally bathed! Let's just give darn high-5's for the basics!"*

I challenge you.

Each one of you, especially you mama's, whether you are busy trying to be everything to everyone else or working to be everything to yourself- compliment a mom today. For any reason at all. Just tell them they are killing it at parenting. Watch the reaction on their pretty faces. What if you are the ONLY person who told them they are doing a good job? That they are more than enough. That might be all they need to get them through their day. It's the little things that make the biggest difference.

(Thank you, Jen Hatmaker, Rachel Hollis, Shasta Nelson, Brené Brown, and my personal friends and family who shared their stories with me.)

Hold Up. There's More

I received so much appreciative the feedback from the "mom-shaming" journal when I posted it to my Facebook group, *Woe Is Not Me*. It's always funny for me to see which of my posts will trigger people's emotions and it's not usually the ones I expect. I actually rewrote and rearranged that one at least ten times. I couldn't quite get it where I wanted it.

Finally, I just decided to put it out there. Stop rewriting and editing it looking for perfection. Ironic, huh? Judging myself and deeming my own work as "not good enough" on a post that was about feeling "good enough." Yet, another example of art imitating life with its sneaky humor.

Once again, I had to remind myself that vulnerability breeds courage. Shame breeds anger. I much prefer feeling brave over feeling anger, right? Perfection is an image, a falsehood, smoke and mirrors. My goal is always to write and share authentically.

Every mom (and dad for that matter) I know loves their children from their tiny toenails, painted or not, all the way to the hairs on the tips of their heads (no matter how small the head and hairs may be.

I don't know one mom who would not crawl to the ends of the earth for their little people, sacrificing their personal, professional or girl time at each turn. But here's the thing, not forming and fostering these friendships is actually harmful to your health!

"Women put it in an optional category. We don't have time for it because we are so busy." (Jen Hatmaker)

But research proves that having friends does not ADD stress to your life, it buffers your body FROM stress! Isn't that amazing? Supportive friendships protect your body from taking on damaging stress. We all know stress can kill you, but your body uses your state of mind to protect you from the physical symptoms of stress. Why are so many women succeeding with businesses from their home? They have created a support system, as well as a business! More women are taking care of themselves in more ways than one.

"Friendship is, by definition, any relationship where both parties feel SEEN in a SAFE and SATISFYING way." Shasta Nelson, Frientimacy)

Meaning you are able to be vulnerable (Seen) while building trust or history together (Safe) in a positive way (Satisfying). So, join something! Schedule it! Get that coffee, glass of wine, hike, or craft activity on your calendar THIS month! Seen. Safe. Satisfying. Your health literally depends on it!

I have found this at my gym. A group of ladies who are of all ages, backgrounds, abilities and talents have made me feel seen, safe and satisfied. Because of this, it's one of the few places I am comfortable wearing a headband and not a hat. Which, for me, has been an internal struggle of insecurity. It is NO coincidence that my physical and mental health have improved. This is not Voodoo magic, guys. This is science. From actual scientists, not just a girl who loves to write about feelings.

(Special thanks, again to Jen Hatmaker's podcast "For the Love- Girlfriends Rule the World".)

Ode to the Land

Forget what you THINK you might know about Cleveland. Turn your head to the negative press. Shake off the heartbreaking news trends that often label this city. There is so much more to this town than what you may think.

I'm beginning to think that God moved us all the way across the country, only to move us to Cleveland, Ohio. Yes, from our home of forever in Columbus, off to a whirl wind adventure in beautiful, Southern California- to Cleveland. I know, it sounds funny to me, too. Until I moved here. Even recently while visiting another city, someone asked, *"Huh, Cleveland. So, how do you like that?"*. Mind you, he asked me with a sneaky smirk, borderline insulting tone as if waiting for me to go off about The Land. I proudly announced that I'd only lived here for a year or so.

And I couldn't be happier about it.

I'm no idiot. The mountains, ocean and blue skies of Orange County are no joke- beyond beautiful. A quick drive to the mountains for skiing and ending the day at the beach is an incredible way to live. We soaked up every minute of each sunrise because we knew it was temporary. As much as we loved it, we never felt at "home".

Why do we love this city so intensely? The people. The doctors. The family. The friends. All providing me with the perfect armor when I would need it the most.

Although, I would not have the humidity out west, I also would not have the medical brilliance of my team at the Cleveland Clinic. As much as I miss my canyon walks, I would not have my family just two hours away. But my biggest surprise of the move, is how far I've fallen in with some of the best people. Yes, yes, I know there are good people everywhere. I know this because I have met some of them. A few of my west coast favorites have been a huge support for me.

But Midwest values are alive and well. There is SO much good out there. People are still selfless. Parents are still raising kind kids. Community members will still go out of their way for their neighbor. We are all going to be okay. At least in Cleveland.

From last minute pizza after soccer games, to taking advantage of 'Kids eat free night' at the local tavern, our friends have really taken us in. Carpools, random play dates, moms checking on moms so we don't lose our minds- People here will pick up your slack when you need a break for no reason other than it's the right thing to do.

A little break down at the gym? Or hesitation to even show up in that damn ball cap? No worries. We've got you, here in Cleveland. An encouraging word, a supportive text, no one fights alone here in Cleveland. Maybe it's because we are experienced with heartbreak. It's because of this heartbreak, these people are empathetic, supportive, proud and everything you want your children to be.

Rough day? Keep your chin up. Because there's a good chance someone will invite you to an Indians game, or even away for a girl's weekend with some sunshine. (True story. This is my week!)

My Ode to Cle, where they smile at you and mean it, where they ask how you are doing and actually want to know. Where they make you feel at home.

Even now, when my personal storm is full blown, I am surrounded by an army. An actual village, ready to take action. Prepared to fight the fight by my side or join me for a celebration drink. So, forget what the media may say about Cleveland, THIS is the real city. These are the real people. This is my home and I will "Defend the Land" to anyone.

Chapter Nine: Mindful in the Midst of Chaos

Mindful? Maybe

You all know that I am willing to try just about anything to bring relief to chronic illness.

I am fortunate enough to have access to an incredible Rheumatologist at the Cleveland Clinic by the name of Leonard Calabrese, DO. (This place is an actual machine and definitely a bragging right for The Land.) He believes there are other things occurring beyond the arthritis diagnosis and is thorough and determined to get to the bottom of me being an autoimmune anomaly. (He agreed this is an accurate term for me after diving into my thick pile of medical records. And he appreciates my sarcastic tone. So, I love him.)

He is the first, of many specialists, to suggest mindfulness and meditation. I realize some of you think I'm nuts. Those of you who have been with me for a while have seen me post about downing fish oil from the bottle, drinking apple cider vinegar, my surplus of supplements, living gluten free, pushing it physically and my belief in essential oils. If nothing else, I'm game for anything.

And the truth is, I feel physically better than I've felt in at least five years and I'm on the lowest dose of prescription medication. So, if this man, a certified genius I'm sure, suggests there's a lot of research behind how mindfulness lowers stress and increases your immune system while lowering inflammation- Let's do it. After all, I've never heard anyone say "Ugh, that meditation has given me migraines." Or, "I'm just so mindful, that it's given me a sinus infection." What do I have to lose? (For the record, he did comment that my mindful state was very positive and genuine and that he appreciates my eagerness to try anything. See why I like him so much?)

But where, oh, where do you begin such an endeavor? Drinking something gross is one thing, but this "mindful" concept takes time and practice. Research even. Mostly, it takes a lot of work. Whew. I don't know, man. I don't know. Then, like a sign from the universe, the day after my appointment, I was able to create a path. You see, one of my fitness instructors actually referenced a book she had just started on being mindful and meditation. SERIOUSLY. The next day! She used the same words as my new favorite doctor during spin class!

So, I took the hint and asked for the name of the book. Two days later (thank you Amazon Prime, I love you more than I love some people) I ordered *Breathe, Mama, Breathe, 5-minute Mindfulness for Busy Mamas* by Shonda Moralis and had the book in hand! Great! Let's be mindful! OMMMMMMMMMM

Then a day passed.
Then two more.
Then another. Shit.

But I'll have you know I have committed to the book for the last three days! The book says to give yourself credit for making it a priority. So, good job, me! I'm trying to do the work. I really am. One slow exhale at a time. And I have to admit that it's much more work than drinking a magic potion.

Do any of you practice Mindfulness or Meditation? Have you tried? Do you think it's a little crazy? Do you refer to it as woo woo, like I often do? Maybe you're thinking I'm a little crazy? Do you have any tips for a wondering mind besides *Go back to the breath*? As I meditated today, I found myself thinking, *Oh, I have to tell my instructor that I'm doing this!*. Yeah, you're not supposed to let your mind do things like that. It's a constant conversation with myself to redirect my thoughts. But...I'm working on it.

Double Mindful

Not only am I mindful today. I am DOUBLE mindful!

That's right, folks. Double the mindful, double the benefits? Um, not sure about that one, yet. But I did participate in my weekly yoga, and then went home for my daily mindful reading and five-minute meditation.

Now, before you reign me as "Queen of Calm," I find myself focusing on the fitness part of yoga rather than the mindful part. Do you guys do this? It's hard to "clear my mind," when I am bending in Cirque du Soleil type positions and trying to keep my eye on the instructor as the miniature thimbles chime in the background in unison with some man chanting "ommmmm." I do love myself a solid savasana. (And then the instructors sweet, little daughter started throwing up in the childcare room, so she had to leave. And she's awesome, by the way.)

So, I came home. Found a comfortable, designated, mindful space. Put on the Meditation Station I found on Pandora. I highly recommend using a station like this if you are attempting this at home. It really helps set the tone! That is, until the "My Pillow" guy chimes in (because I refuse to pay for Pandora) telling you how to get the "deep, peaceful, REM sleep you need for your health and energized days." But, mind over matter, as they say. I redirected my attention, my breath and set the timer for five minutes. Just five minutes. You can do anything for five minutes, right? I love it when people say things like that. I always think, well I couldn't hold my breath for five minutes, or a squat or handstand for that matter. But I do love a good challenge, so this I'm willing to try.

While feeling the Zen powers ease in to my surprisingly relaxed muscles, I began to notice things:

The air vent next to my bed makes a weird whistling/humming sound. Has it always made that sound or am I just noticing it? Is that normal? I should tell my husband.

Ooops- redirect my focus.

My sweet dog snuggled next to me has a nasty odor and desperately needs a bath. But I hate giving her a bath in the middle of winter. It was easier in California because she could dry off outside.

Damn it! Focus, Angie. Focus on the breath.

How the hell do we have an inch of snow on the ground? Wasn't it just fifty degrees and my son took his shirt off while jumping on the trampoline? Seriously, Ohio.

UH! Lost that focus again. Close your eyes. Don't look at the timer. Don't look at the timer!

Crap.

I looked the timer. Cheater. Only three more seconds. Whew.

So, not a huge success I suppose. However, not a failure either. I did it and it does make me feel good. Even if I'm not totally doing it right. I'll keep at it.

"Offer yourself more permission to simply be." -Shonda Moralis (Breathe, Mama, Breathe.)

Namaste"ish". Almost.

Forgetful Mindful

Yup. It's happened. I completely forgot to be mindful and meditate today.

I'd like to think it was because I was so calm and Zen-like that my body just didn't need it, but that would be a lie. I simply forgot and went about my day with the usual mom duties.

To be honest, I did think about it once. However, I decided to eat carrot cake and watch Ellen instead. In my defense, I felt very aware of my feelings while eating the carrot cake. And they were calm, happy feelings. I guess in some way Ellen and carrot cake are a lot like meditation. They put me in a happy place.

Maybe I'm not so good at this.

But tomorrow. For sure tomorrow. I'll be more mindful than ever before. Tomorrow. Meditation will happen. Tomorrow. Yes, sir.

Tonight, I'm tired and just finished season one of "The Marvelous Mrs. Maisel" (side note- awesome show on Amazon Prime) so I'm going to bed now.

Mindful in Vegas

Well, some not-so shocking news here. I spent last week in Vegas and meditated a grand total of ZERO times! You would think that, of all places, the city of sin is the EXACT place in need some mindfulness. I saw a lot of questionable people making questionable choices without a concern for mindfulness. And apparently, I blended right in. Hopefully, not with all of Vegas. Maybe not the smelly guy dressed up like the lead singer from KISS, or the other one dressed up like Bumble Bee from the Transformers. Although I love a good costume party, I was meaning that my mind blended in with the hustle and bustle of the city that never sleeps.

To my defense, I did pack my meditation guide book in my carryon AND even took it out at the hotel once or twice. But that was it. I'm sure the cleaning crew at the hotel was thinking, "Wow, this lady must be dripping in Zen and oozing calmness. Good for her." More likely they didn't think anything about it at all. Can you imagine the things hotel crews find? They could make a reality show.

Ha. We all know better. (More likely dripping in anxiety and oozing sarcasm.)

Because life is chaotic. Because things are a bit messy right now. And because my head is still swimming in Vegas lights, magic shows, time changes and Justin Timberlake music, I hit it hard today. (Can you hit meditation hard? Is it possible to aggressively meditate?)

The chapter I read today, from *Breathe, Mama, Breathe*, was about taking a "SNAP Break," basically taking a quick "pause" before you snap at your kids, spouse or family members. Saying that I CAN relate to this is like saying the Kardashian's love the spotlight. No kidding.

Stop.
Notice.
Accept.

Angie Gleine

Pay attention to your breath.

The author does this alone time in her closet which I love so much and makes me want to have coffee with her because I can so relate. If you love being a mom all the time or thrive off of life's daily stresses, keep getting it! But I am a human who often slips off to a quiet closet, talks to herself out loud, and whispers bad words under her breath, or loudly if no one is around.

I snap.

So, for the benefit of those who love me, even those who don't, a SNAP break is a survival strategy for our home because I'd like to keep these people around!

Things I noticed:
- I had an easier time with my breath. I could feel it down in my belly, but not yet able to send it to my fingers and toes like suggested. (How exactly does one get air into toes?)
- My hands felt really heavy, almost like weights. (Pretty sure this means I was really relaxed which is an improvement.)
- My mind is full. Full of distractions from to-do lists to the sound of my dog pacing in the hallway. (Which reminded me of her faint limp and that she turns fourteen at the end of the month which is really old for my pup, etc.)
- CONSTANT redirection to the damn breath. (It's like having your kids do homework while watching YouTube and eating cupcakes with sprinkles.) I've got some work to do here.
- A blanket of gratitude. Sounds strange, but I just had a strong sense of being grateful. (I liked this.)

And when it was over, I felt good. I just felt good.

Puppies

Ever tried doing your morning mindful/meditation time with an eight-week-old puppy?

Don't.

Don't. Even. Bother.

Ommmm

Start each day with a grateful heart. Riighttt.

This picture makes me laugh so hard. As a wise friend, once wrote "I cannot type this without laughing" in regard to an obviously sarcastic comment she made. How did your day REALLY start, my friends? Were you all *Ommm* and finding the beauty in the trees dancing in the wind?

I was not.

My day started with a 2:00 and 6:00AM barking call from the sweet pup. Quickly followed by discovering my son was sleeping on the couch which forced me to be extra quiet when desperately searching for my coffee fixings. My daughter begging to watch something stupid on YouTube and my husband remained peacefully snoring.

My monkeys. My early morning circus.

Is that more realistic for you? Don't be fooled, people. A picture on social media can be awfully misleading. I love being real. Being real is so much more fun. Because life is so damn funny when you think about it. After being up for three hours and several cups of coffee, I am now ready to start my day with a grateful heart.

Tales from A Mediocre Meditating Mother

I thought I was a meditation mom drop-out! It turns out, there are so many ways to meditate. It's really about what brings you to your happy place. And I don't mean the mall or an empty bottle of wine! Although, that's always a tempting option. But I'm really trying to focus on putting good things in my body and mind and not just temporary fixes.

> "So, you can see that any activity that brings us into deeper communion with our real self in the present moment, whatever gives you a sense of peaceful unity, is a moving meditation. With the right frame of mind, the right view, and the right attitude, we can move as one with our inner self at all times, thereby creating harmony, beauty, peace, right action, and love right where we are, right now." (Moralis, Breathe, Mama, Breathe)

This. This I can do. This is real life meditation. This is good.

I find myself doing Moving Meditation at spin class when I'm pushing up a heavy hill, feeling the lyrics to the steady beat, usually chanting a mantra in my head. It goes between *We can do hard things*, or *God is with her she cannot fail*. I totally recommend finding a quote or a verse that speaks to you. You'd be surprised how often you need it.

I do this when I'm cooking a favorite recipe with a glass of wine and singing along with my dear friend, Alexa. (She's basically a family member at this point and is responsible for getting us to school on time!) While the family is gathered around either helping me prep dinner, or completing homework, it's a good time to talk a minute and soak it in. I pause, breath, look around and appreciate the moment.

I feel this sense of calm when snuggled up with my kids after a shower, when they are so fresh and so clean clean. As parents we know these moments are fleeting so we soak them in just a little deeper. We let go of the sibling's fights and the heaviness of life. Somehow once everyone is snuggled with a TV show or a book, you forget any frustration you had throughout the evening routine. It slips away with each rise and fall of their chest.

Breathing in the good stuff and taking that pause to just be still and appreciate it. That's a meditation I can get behind.

Morning Ritual

Anyone who is into any type of self-improvement, professional development or is up to date on the latest books and podcasts, is aware of the focus on gratitude. It's everywhere and it's everything if you are looking to live a fulfilling life of happiness. And I know, I know, it can sound a little woo woo. I am a skeptic of anything too touchy feely. But the fact that I keep seeing gratitude in my favorite books, from my favorite authors and podcasts has made me rethink so many things. So, stick with me if you're skeptical. Hear me out and don't turn the page just yet.

For starters, I in no way plan to constantly look around and be grateful for every little thing every minute of the day. That's not realistic. Putting a hashtag on it, does not make it authentic. (Thank you very much generation #blessed.) Living a life of gratitude is much more work than a hashtag. But I won't get started on that because that's not the point.

I met up with some high school friends at a girlfriends' house in Worthington, Ohio for our annual Christmas dinner. (Side note, how cool is it that twenty years after graduation we still get together? We tell the best old stories and updated each other on recent events. It's easy, breezy and wonderful. It's very cool, I tell ya.) I was complimented on how great I looked. I'm pointing this out for a very specific reason, not out of vanity. People were not struck by my rocking body or designer clothes. Keep in mind I'm almost forty and let's be real, I buy my clothes from Marshalls and Target. There was something else about me that struck them besides my new pixie cut. Obviously, they were very sweet about my hair situation and have been supportive from the get-go. But on separate points in the evening, I was told that I just looked great. Something about me seemed different. Something about the way I was carrying myself, more confident, surer. There may have been talk of a bit of glow about me! No, I'm not pregnant, not that kind of glow. I was told that from the minute I walked through the door, I carried around a different vibe. In the best way possible.

You know what that difference was? I bet you can guess; Happiness. Joy.

And you know what I read from John O'Leary? *"You can't have joy without gratitude."* You need both. Like with suffering and victory. They just go together. Two peas in a pod. There is scientific research on this. That is why so many professionals are talking about gratitude. It leads to joy. Practicing gratitude each day wires your brain to be joyful. It shifts your brain to look for the good. Isn't that incredible? We can retrain our brains to literally see life differently! I mean, my goodness. That's powerful stuff. And SO doable. If you're willing to put in the work. Like with anything good, it all comes back to putting in the work.

Even Brene Brown, in YEARS of research, discovered that *"The men and women who most fully lean in to joy were those who practiced gratitude."* It just makes so much damn sense, you guys. Get yourself on the grateful train!

Not sure how? Let me tell you, it's easy if you're willing to put in the TIME. In the time I've dedicated to practicing gratitude, I have rewired my brain faster than I have potty-trained the puppy. For me, and many others, it's all about the morning routine. You HAVE to make it part of your morning routine. Rachel Hollis (Girl, Wash Your Face) and her husband do this each day. A new podcast I've been into, Ryan Niddel's 15 Minutes to Freedom, also talks about the importance of your morning ritual. Each of these successful entrepreneurs emphasize the importance of waking up early and practicing gratitude.

You prepare your body by dressing for the weather. You prepare yourself by fueling your body with coffee and food. You do things in order to be ready for the day, right? So, why aren't you preparing your mind? Why aren't you arming yourself? Practicing gratitude early in the morning is the BEST way to arm yourself before you walk out that door. Before your feet even hit the floor, did you express gratitude for that opportunity?

When you shower. When you lay in bed thinking about the day ahead of you. When you brush your teeth or pour that first cup of coffee. These are all times you can focus on the good stuff in your life.

I recommend finding a quiet space while the morning is still and before chaos and responsibility ensues, to sit and reflect. If you love to write, then write. There are numerous gratitude journals available right now. If you just like sitting, then just sit. But give yourself five to thirty minutes to focus on the good. It can be simple like hot water, a cozy bed, or a delicious cup of coffee. Or, you can think about the people and pets in your life. It does NOT matter! But I promise you, your body will physically recognize the calm and your mind will take note. For me, it's a cup of coffee, the glow of the Christmas tree, and everyone still sleeping. Sometimes I write, sometimes I simply think and watch it snow. (Because that happens a lot when you live in the snow belt.)

Then later in the day when life happens, because life ALWAYS happens. Something will go wrong. Someone will piss you off. Things won't go as planned. But you know what's great? You're armed for that. You are prepared for the unexpected. Your brain is trained to slow down, breathe, and handle that shit. You are armed to NOT lose your shit.

Now, don't get me wrong, we are all human and will absolutely lose our minds from time to time. I lost it last Tuesday when my kids continued to ignore my four hundred and eighty-seven requests to brush their teeth before school. I screamed, I rioted, I lost my damn mind. Oh, well. Better luck the next time. Because on THIS morning, when my eight-year-old continued to tell me that I do NOT know how to spell "squeak" and I had told him how to spell it incorrectly all while screaming and breaking a pencil, I kept my cool. Thank you very much. I was armed after doing my morning ritual of quiet gratitude. I took a breath, calmly walked away and let him know that I was happy to help him, but I was not going to be talked to that way. I ended it with "Good luck on your spelling test." And he huffed off to brush his teeth. A year ago, I would have let that boy hear all about my bachelor's degree from the University of Dayton and a master's degree from THE Ohio State University. I would have gone on and on until he was paying zero attention and then taken away food and tv for the weekend. (Because I had lost my damn mind.) I just have no idea where he gets his temper?

Here's the thing. I feel good. Like, really good. Yes, I have weird hair. Yes, I'm not sure what I'm doing with parenting and my husband and I don't always see eye to eye. Even then, I am actually filled with joy. I walk around each day and think, "How the hell did I get so damn lucky?" I get emotional just thinking about my life. Like a teary-eyed Hallmark actress. I'm so damn lucky

But you know what else I am? I am a fighter, and I have put in the effort every single day to be grateful. I have made the CHOICE to work on my mind. Through reflecting, reading, listening. I put in the work every day, not with hashtags, with my life. And it has made all the difference.

Oops. I Did It Again

Wow.

Ok.

So, it's been a bit. I think I got sucked that in to that vortex of being everything for everyone and forgetting to be everything to myself. It's a dangerous place, that vortex. But the kids needed valentines, and there were thousands of basketball tournaments, right? My husband has a very stressful job and apparently everyone in my house likes eating food and wearing clean clothes. Also, no one else wants to walk the dog, even though it is on record that everyone promised they would.

That's what happens so often with us, doesn't it? Whether it's our nutrition, fitness, organization, self-care, whatever the healthy habit may be is pushed to the side. Like my daughter does with her carrots at dinner. Like we're thinking, *Oh, I'll get to that later. Let me just take care of a few more things first.*" And then those few things turn into saying "yes" for things you don't actually have time for, and everyone else's needs being met EXCEPT yours. And that is when things start to crumble. You refocus your energy to get back to your healthy routine and then BAM! That tug of war rope enters the equation. Someone needs this, volunteer for that, a little person is struggling with blank, fractions start coming home for homework, etc. life happens.

And none of it is bad, none of it is that hard and mostly it's really nice to live in a community that leans on each other. But, that's also what makes it so easy to say "sure", "you've got it" and "yes". It's not about being selfish. It's about the fact that, little by little, I allow myself to disappear. I turn to more Bravo TV, less reading, more scrolling, less writing. It's about me and my choices. I'm fortunate enough to have a team, but it can often feel like I'm carrying my team on my back. (Which is not good for arthritis in more ways than one!)

The good news? I've been here before and I recognize the symptoms my body is showing me. The fingers on my right hand begin to curve a bit more as my arthritis talks to me. I get knocked down with a serious sinus infection which I may have mistaken as the bubonic plague. A tight knot develops at the base of my rib cage, just above my belly, creating a nice little shelter for my stress to hibernate in. I also notice a tightness in my hip flexors, which is a popular place for women to hold tension. There're symptoms more obvious to the outside world like my short temper, comfort food cravings and occasional snappy judgement in my head. My body is literally screaming at me to STOP being everything to everyone and attempting to remind me that I need to be everything to myself first. Get back to writing, meditation, nutrition and reading. Reach out to the people to who hold me accountable and remind me of my worth.

This does not mean to stop taking care of my family and responsibilities, you guys. I don't mean to throw all responsibilities to the wind and live on a deserted island with Paco for a few months. (Although that does sound tempting at times. Whoever Paco is.) It's a reminder that my body needs me to carve out that time for myself. Wake up earlier, sit in silence at pick-up, grab coffee with a friend and have that hard conversation with a loved one. These are things that literally heal my body and mind, which then makes me a much nicer human.

I've returned to myself care routine for the last four days and I can literally visualize the knot in my belly shrinking. There is a calmness returning to my tone and breath. I can handle when that tug-of-war rope enters the room, when my husband has a rough day, or when the kids are struggling with homework. I can breathe in the opportunities of a new day and breath out the early morning arthritic pains and challenges that will come. But I can only do this well if I agree to be everything to myself first.

Take care of yourself so that we can take care of each other.

Chapter Ten: Fitness Will Not Kill You...Mostly

Confession Time

I t wasn't pretty. But I did it.

I have a confession. I am one of those people who like to work out. I know. It's annoying. You might be rolling your eyes right now, but at least I own it. You won't see me fishing for a compliment by claiming I never workout. That would be annoying and untrue. For me, as for most, fitness has a direct effect on my head space.

Much like you, there is so much of my life that is NOT in my control. I've recently discovered that I may have some controlling tendencies. Laugh all you want. I am doing my best to own this one too. It has been brought to my attention that I like to control situations, classrooms, children, outcomes, etc. The children one is really tough. I just don't understand why they don't know where their shoes are! Or, why they would not want to brush their teeth and listen to the teacher. Honestly, what so hard about that?! Ugh. I digress.

As I slowly come to terms with my controlling habits, I am looking for the beauty of letting go. I cannot always control my health; children, employment, but I CAN control my choices. It took me three decades and counting to get to this point.

Autoimmune diseases make you feel anything but strong. They make you feel weak and powerless, unable to control which part of your body is going to fail you next. As my physical health improved a few years ago, so did my mental health. It was like a switch flipped saying, *Oh, wait, I am strong enough to do this. I have fought bigger battles than this.*

Life was good, until it wasn't. You know what I mean?

As autoimmune diseases often cycle, the meds that had been keeping me afloat were no longer effective. My feet and hands started showing signs of inflammation first, then the other joints decided to join in the party. By "party" I mean, "let's get swollen to the point that we can't even bend!" So, likely not the kind of party you want to attend even if it has great food and drinks. With the immobility comes the pain. I could compare it to daggers and arrows being shot through you in sharp movements. But then there's also the constant throbbing pain to help balance out the party. You know, the more the merrier, right? It's a hell of a bash.

As my doc and I worked to start a new treatment plan, I had to stop all physical exercise. This even included walking down stairs, putting a shirt over my head and squeezing a tube of toothpaste, because apparently the "party" was just raging. My joints were throwing one fierce fiesta.

It's been four months since I have been able to exercise. Four months since I have felt STRONG and in control of my body. I had to let that shit go. I was patient, and kind to my body, and followed the doctor's orders.

But today, my friends, today I headed back to the gym.

I was terrified. Like a new kid walking into the cafeteria. Stomach flopping all around, wanting to turn around, but knowing this was something I had to do. I had to start somewhere. I had to start here. I chose PIYO because if I could be in love with a fitness routine, it would be PIYO. Honestly, if I could marry PIYO, I would. It's beautiful and powerful and STRONG. (Which are all of the things I want to be anyway!) Plus, my amazing instructor at **24-Hour Fitness, Anaheim Hills**, Larisa Settembro, throws in all my jams with the perfect amount of humor and positive vibes. She's the real deal. I'm talking world class fitness instructor, here.

As the music came on, it felt like coming home. Granted it was a messy, chaotic home. It was like when you come back from vacation and things are a little dusty and stuffy. Your clothes and extra towels are thrown about from packing, however, it's comfortable and it's all yours. It just feels good. That's the warm and cozy feeling I had when JT's voice started, and my energy level jumped one thousand notches. (Don't even pretend you can't sing along to "Can't Stop the Feeling" by Justin Timberlake on a Friday morning.)

And, you guys. I was KILLING it. I mean, I had that "good song in my pocket" and all the moves coming back to me like an old friend. I OWNED that five-minute warm-up like a BOSS!

And then, well, it got ugly. Really ugly.

Damn. I thought it would feel good. But the truth is, it sucked. I didn't feel good AT ALL. I was shaking, sweaty, nauseous and light-headed. I even had to stop a few times to stop the world from spinning. In no way did I feel strong or powerful in my movements. It was more of, *this sucks…what am I doing here?* Four or five times I actually told myself to *SHUT UP!*

"Be patient and gentle with yourself," I whispered while my arms and legs shook like a leaf. But I finished. And as I walked to my car on unsteady legs, the tears fell. I may not have been as strong or graceful as I had hoped, but I thought back to August when I could not literally dress myself. How I scooted down the stairs because I physically could not bend my legs enough to walk down them.

I showed up. I CHOSE to get back at it, as ugly and sloppy as it may have been. I did it and I will make the choice to show up and do the work every, damn time.

Taking Names and Throwing Punches

Oh, yeah. This. Is. Happening. I'm taking names, dropping mics and throwing punches. I'm BACK baby!

Week five is currently taking place in my attempt to take-back-the-gym. I've worked out five to six days each week for the first time since June. (For those of you rolling your eyes , just stop. No time for haters here.) This RA medical nonsense has been a pain in the arse. Maybe more likely my back, hands, knees, hips and feet, but you get the idea. Meds are a life saver, a game changer, a miracle worker. However, it is incredibly annoying to be so damn patient with your body. 'Ain't nobody got time for that!

But it is what it is.

You do what you've got to do.

You have to keep showing up for yourself

I've been very busy being patient and then pissed. Patient and then pissed some more.

"Every day, every hour, turn that pain into power." ~The Script.

Because of that, I've been able to reduce the number of meds I take, including the lowest does of prednisone in nine months. Which is still too much, and it's kind of a miracle I don't speak at the same octave as James Earl Jones.

I've also researched and increased my NATURAL supplements which included drastically reducing/eliminating diary and processed sugar. Dairy, fine. Whatever.

Cheese is the hardest to cut. Almond milk is decent enough to work with, as well as almond creamer. Sugar though...

I can now drink coffee, although only one cup. I am focusing on what I am putting in my body. I've said it before, and I'll say it without hesitation...IT MATTERS!

So, don't be surprised when you see me bench pressing cars or doing one arm push-ups. (Well, maybe a little surprised.)

Don't tell me I won't. Don't tell me I can't. I've got plans and I feel DAMN good! I'm sucker punching arthritis. I know it will be there. I feel it in every joint, every day. But, right now, I am winning.

Yes. You. Can.

3.3 miles. BOOM. Practically a marathon, right?

This past week I went running for the first time since July. I know some of my running friends can run three miles with zero sleep and hung over. But I am NOT one of those people. (Plus, we've got crazy hills in the California canyons.) Never have been. Never will be. At least, not the natural ease some runners have.

It may have been the apple cider vinegar. It may have been the view. It could have been the Lady Gaga mix with a side of Britney Spears. It could have also been that I imagined Margie Huber Belair and Christopher William were running next to me. In my head we were having great conversations about former students who don't know how to use paperclips (true story) and an up-coming wedding. It's possible I laughed at our imaginary chat leaving anyone else out for a jog very confused about who I was talking with. Margie and Chris are good friends of mine who are, in fact, natural runners. Annoyingly so. But being teachers proves they are some of the best people you will meet. They are the ones who supported my first 5K and then ran the "Buckeye 4 Miler" with me where we got to finish in the Horseshoe at The Ohio State University. In real life they are able to hold whole conversations while running miles at a time under nine minutes. Meanwhile, I bring very little to the conversation table because some of us have to use our breath for actual breathing and focus on not dying.

I MAY have dropped some inappropriate words along the way. I MAY have had a few talks with the man upstairs to get up those hills. I MAY have swallowed a bug. I DEFINITELY wanted to quit.

Either way. WHATEVER it takes.

You CAN push your body further than you think. You CAN go just a little further than you are comfortable with. You ARE so much stronger than you give yourself credit for.

I have never been the most athletic, fastest or strongest athlete. But my WILL is so much more than what you see. And once I got out of my head, I landed in a place of power and possibility. Give it a try.

Feeling Feisty

I set out today to PUSH my body. I'm not looking to sign up for any marathons here, but I wanted to see what this body had in it. Mind you, my hammies are dead from the latest round of Piyo. But I am on my lowest meds since last July, even though I could run a pharmacy out of my purse, and I was feeling feisty.

There's a lot of things I'm NOT. (Timely, soft-spoken and serious- to name a few.) One thing I AM is disciplined and stubborn. Discipline got me to lace up my shoes, turn up my jams, and hit the pavement. I was gliding like a gazelle down my court for a good thirty-two seconds when I felt my discipline weaken. Damn.

However, when discipline slowed. Motivation kicked in. Not just any motivation, but motivation from my friends Salt-n-Peppa telling me that they were HERE! Running alongside me in their multi-colored, polyester jumpsuits. One on each side rapping, "P-P-Push It!" Now that you're all singing it, imagine the seventh grade version of me. Frizzy mall bangs, middle school, awkward skin and overwhelmingly insecure. That's an image for you, huh?

Well THIS time friends, I was proudly rapping along while gasping for air (because I'm very gangster) and possibly doing hand motions all while running like the graceful gazelle that I am. Please know, NONE of this is easy for me. Especially not, the rapping. I am not a naturally athletic person. But I am a disciplined person by choice.

After about five minutes of any cardio workout, the hips fight me, and my hands and feet start to tingle. It's the same sensation as when your feet start to fall asleep. My hands get purple and blotchy in the most glamorous way. Probably happens to all the super models. It lasts the whole workout and usually another thirty minutes after I'm done. It's annoying and likely a side effect of my meds or a nerve issue. (No worries, I have an appointment Thursday.) It's all just par for the course.

But I did it. I got in my 5K and then some with a little more help from Ms. Spears and Usher. My discipline left me feeling damn good! (Minus the tingling going on. So annoying.)

Don't worry about how you look. Forget the fact that you may not be a natural. Just made the decision to do it. Be disciplined to do what you want and then "PUSH IT!"

Let Me Clear My Throat

Do you remember, a few pages back I wrote a cute little thing about how much I loved working out? Yeah, wasn't I just ADORABLE? I'd like to punch that annoying, happy workouty girl right about now. Who was she?

After a three-month hiatus of traveling, three rounds of pneumonia drugs, side effects, settling into a new town...and a healthy dose of French fries, wine and laziness- I'm back in the fitness saddle. (Don't worry, there's a harness for the wine!) Why didn't anyone tell me how hard this is? You all just rolled your eyes and scrolled along while I preached my "It feels so good to be healthy! I am overwhelmed with power and strength!"

Blahhhh....give me a flipping break. It. Completely. Sucks. (Literally sucking wind and red faced.)

I am trying everything that is offered to motivate me. But let me tell you what will take me in the end. Not arthritis, not a car crash, not illness or aging gracefully...Spin Class. Yup. Death by Spin Class. Go ahead and title my biography. Put it in the obituary.

Any spinners out there? Do you ever get to the point where you actually enjoy this slow, cruel, torture? I mean, the hills, the speeding? They shout at you, "Turn it up to 10." And just when you start to get into some sort of comfort level, "Now add push-ups to the hill," they scream! For real?

With my jaw on the handle bars and my eyes bulging out of my head, I look around the room for some support. But, NO. They are all getting their workout on and leaving me in the dust. Even in my fourth week of "trying to live my best life", I can honestly say, I hate it. I mutter curse words under my breath and try to *Be Still* and *Breathe*, while the sweat rushes down around me. All my usual mantras have ZERO influence in the moment. I. Hate. It.

The funny thing is, I keep going back. Somehow, I keep showing up. WTH?

Because the Other Kid Got Hit by a Bus

It's like I have to prove to myself that I CAN, and I WILL conquer spin. That damn Irish stubbornness really has some power behind it. Either that or I suffer from some sort of sick determination not to fail at this.

It's not just me is it? Anyway, I apologize for my "I just love working out" posts. You won't see me pretending to continue my love affair with fitness for a bit. Just going to continue to be honest about it all. And honestly, working out is not my friend at the moment. Even though I'll keep showing up, I'm mostly hoping I don't die on that damn bike. I'm off to bake cookies. (Granted they are gluten and dairy free.) Keeping it real, the honesty and the ingredients.

Return of Spin

You guys. I did it. I went back to spin class and I did not die.

I may have seen glimmers of the "other side," but I did not die. And I didn't hate it. Completely, anyway. I keep going back to the saying coined by Glennon Doyle, "We can do hard things." Isn't that so true? You do hard things all the freaking time, right? And I do hard things. I CHOOSE to keep doing hard things just to prove that I can. Desperate times call for desperate measures, or at least motivational tank tops. I pulled out the tank my husband bought be to wear in my first 5K. It says, "You got this." Because, I do.

Not only did I just show up to class, I was INTO it. For the first time in four weeks of this best life fitness stuff, I was able to keep up with the jumps and push-ups. I may have wobbled. I may have teetered. I was definitely the only one grunting up those hills. (Plus, I went through not one, but two sweat soaked towels. Gross. Someday I should look into my extensive sweating situation.)

But I didn't have to stop.

Slowed, maybe. But didn't stop.

Made incredibly ugly pain stretched faces but didn't stop.

For some reason my brain kept repeating *God is with her, she will not fail.* So, I went with it. I let that feeling take over and just kept pushing. I couldn't keep up with the fifty and sixty-year-old women who were spinning at unearthly speeds. These ladies are tough as nails, sweet as honey and committed to self-improvement. They are the exact people you need by your side at the gym. (If God is with me, some Peloton God's must be with them!)

No matter what my speed may have been. I did not fail.

Before you send me a lifetime membership to Soul Spinners or any other spin club, slow your role and pump the breaks. Just because I didn't hate it once, does not mean I am a committed spinner. This week reminded me that I get a little "high" (notice the quotes) from conquering a challenging that my thirty-seven-year-old, arthritis-stricken body is not supposed to be able to do.

God IS with me; therefore, I will not fail. I will struggle and make strange, ugly noises and faces. But I will not fail. See you later comfort zone. I like where this ride is taking me.

It Doesn't Get Easier. You Get Stronger.

We all do hard things every day. All of us. But I think we have a misconception that it must be easier for some people than others. I used to think that way, too. Until I left my comfort zone in a pile of sweat.

- *Oh, well, she's always been athletic so it's just easier for her to build muscle.*
- *She's so dedicated to eating healthy. I could never do that.*
- *Yeah, that girl loves working out. Must be nice to have it so easy. I'd be in better shape too if I loved working out.*
- *I wish I was a morning person. There's no way I could wake up early each day like that.*
- *She is always so positive, must be nice to be able to look on the bright side all the time.*

Guess what? None of those things are easy. They are all hard to do. And they are hard every single day. While, I am sure there are exceptions to this, most people do not wake up and easily do the above things all with a smile plastered on their faces. Not at all. I don't know ONE person who is always positive, constantly excited to work out and down some quinoa and salmon. Not a one. And I know some amazingly dedicated, inspirational people. One thing these people have done is they've made a choice. They carefully choose what they want their day and their life to look like. And then they do it. Excuse free. (Or, with minor excuses. We are human after all.)

There are a lot of things that are not easy for me. So many. Like, I still overcook chicken more often than not. I usually shrink one of my husband's shirts at least once a week. I'm too sarcastic with my kids on the daily. I sneak gluten. A lot. And working out is REALLY hard. I have never had an easy day at the gym where I didn't have multiple muscles burning, feel a little faint, say a lot of inappropriate things and consider walking out. Sometimes, I get a rush out of it. Sometimes. But each day there are moments that I'm sure I'm close to death and hate life.

It is not easy for me. And it's probably not easy for you. It's okay. Just show up.

I show up because it matters. I show up because, even though it doesn't get easier, I get stronger. When people see me at the gym it might not seem like much, or maybe it does. I don't know. But to me, when I look at my reflection, I see a fighter. I see power and dedication DESPITE the struggle. I see someone down to one mg of prednisone, the lowest in seven years and with a full head of hair. I look at my reflection as if I don't know the person in it, admiring her will to keep pushing through.

And you know what's great about this? It could be you. I know "if I can do it, so can you," is annoyingly overused these days, but it's SO true. It's about making that choice to be THAT girl and then fight like hell for her over and over again.

Take a minute, hell, take seven minutes and think about where you began. I don't know one person who hasn't been through some sort of hell. Reflect on that. I guarantee the version of me two, five or ten years ago would not have looked so confident and empowered in a quick snapshot. Would you?

Another thing that's great about looking at your own reflection? If you don't like it, make a choice. Yes, it's going to be hard. Duh. Get over it. Get on with it. It's not ever going to be easy, but you are going to be so damn strong. Then when you look back on that snap shot, you'll think, "that's me?". Holy shit.

There may not be puppies and rainbows falling from the sky, but the self-acceptance that comes with it is so much better. Because it's real. It keeps you fired up for another day and will rub off on the people in your life. Be prepared to fight. Be prepared to doubt yourself throughout it all. Be prepared to take a few steps back and then forward again. After that, be prepared to see yourself becoming someone even more powerful than you knew existed. Surprise yourself with your strength.

Acknowledgements

It was a girl's trip in September of 2018 when a few special ladies and I poured out our hopes, fears over cocktails. It wasn't the first time I was told that I needed to share my story, but it was the first time I trusted it. It was the real first step toward listening to my inner voice which had been telling me for years to *Do It*. Ali and Colleen, thank you for pushing me when I needed pushed, encouraging me when I was in doubt and holding me accountable when I was overwhelmed. You two and the devoted ladies at Wembley have given me a home where I'm accepted, supported and empowered. You all have saved my life, or at least helped me see mine more clearly. My world is better because of all of you proving that what you say and do matters. I'm so fortunate to have had the little bubble of the St. Joan of Arc and Kenston communities wrap their arms around my family since the minute we arrived. They were the exact people we needed at the precise time we needed them. They are the best of the best.

Beyond my time here in Cleveland, I am very fortunate to have been surrounded by some of the best people since my middle school days. David, Krista, Tara, Megan and Lori, I treasure our years of *Monthly Dinners*, turned into *Annual Christmas Dinners*. The numerous texts, ridiculous laughter and countless conversations proving that time and miles do not dictate our level of support. I would travel down memory lane with you all any day of the week.

My loyal Reynoldsburg co-workers Margie, Lynne and Chris who inspire me as much now as they did in my teaching days. We may have met as "work friends", but quickly and fiercely developed a bond over paperclip usage, Toto and Bobbi Kristina Brown. We are four puzzle pieces with our own curves and grooves yet fit together like a perfect compliment. Thank you for being exactly who you are and accepting me as one of the pieces.

Jaime and Nikki, my partners in crime. The three of us could literally take a girl's trip to hell and back and find a way to laugh our way through it, somehow coming out stronger in the end. Thank you for a friendship that allows us to be brutally honest and completely breakdown yet never question if someone has our back. Some things in this life waver or shake: we do not.

I know it sounds cliché to write "I would not be where I am today," but without the inspirational and hardworking team at the Cleveland Clinic, it is a fact. The level of professionalism combined with compassion is everything a hospital system should strive to be. My grateful heart and strong body would not be defying the odds without doctors like Leonard Calabrese, DO and Angela Kyei, MD. Not only are these two respected experts in their field, they are willing to sit patiently with me. These doctors listen, encourage and empower me as a human first, medical case second. They are up-to-date- on the latest medical trends and open to the healing powers of our natural world. Dr. Calabrese and Dr. Kyei were exactly where I needed them to be when I needed it. They represent a different level of professionalism.

To the people who write, share and speak with vulnerability. Whether it's through books, podcasts or music, you continue to prove that words matter. Your courage to put your own vulnerability into the world allows people like me to feel connected, heard and accepted. You are gently proving to society that being vulnerable also means being brave. People like Glennon Doyle, John O'Leary, Brené Brown have opened the door and invited us to let go of our idea of perfect and learn to love ourselves. It's a whole new world on the other side and I'm so glad I've walked through that door to join them.

My sweet, sarcastic, unbelievably loving and complicated family. People request a diagram to keep up with our modern ways. But the truth is, it's the whole mixed-up, messy lot of you who make me who I am. The steps, halves, in-laws and beyond have given me various insights and opinions. And the luckiest part? Every one of these people love me. I literally have support from every dynamic and end of the country that a person can have. I could not have hand-picked a more supportive, generous and hysterical group of people. I will forever be the luckiest girl in the world because of the people who raised and grew up with me. To my parents, who will often see their mistakes rather than their successes. I hope you read this and take a minute to know you did this, too. I have never fought alone and any mistake you thought you made led us to this wonderful life we are living.

Chip and my kids. Holy moly. We've really been through it, haven't we? I purposely did not share much of our story because I hold it too close to my heart and it's not just mine to share. We've had days when we threw our hands in the air, yet still found magic hidden in the little things. We don't always do or say the right things, but we do always work our way back to each other. Every day we choose our life. We choose each other. We choose to never give up. Together, we have designed a life we love. You three are the reason I find joy in each day.

I did it, Grandmom. I really did it. I felt you every step of the way. I heard your voice and saw your face. I always have.

Correction: We did it. All of us.

Contact Information

Want to reach out to the author or follow her on social media?

Find her using the following contacts:
- Facebook public group "Whoa is Not me"
- Instagram @stone_and_sarcasm
- Email: angiegleine@yahoo.com

Made in the USA
Columbia, SC
22 August 2019